Bible

Crafts & More

AGES 6-8

Standard
PUBLISHING
Bringing The Word to Life

Cincinnati, Ohio

DEDICATION

This book is dedicated to Kathy and Dana Calhoun.
May God's blessings and abundant life fill your days. Thank you for being a godly example
and encouragement of faith.

Bible Crafts & More (Ages 6-8)

This book is a revision of *Bible Crafts & More for Ages 4–8,* © 1999.

All Scripture quotations, unless otherwise indicated, are taken from the HOLY BIBLE® NEW INTERNATIONAL VERSION® NIV®.
Copyright 1973, 1978, 1984 by International Bible Society. Used by permission of Zondervan. All rights reserved.

Credits
Crafts: Nancy I. Sanders
Cover design: Liz Malwitz
Interior design: Scott Ryan
Inside illustrations: Lynne Davis
Project editors: Christine Spence and Chris Wallace
Acquisitions editor: Ruth Frederick

Standard Publishing, Cincinnati, Ohio.
A division of Standex International Corporation.
© 2005 by Standard Publishing
All rights reserved.
Printed in the United States of America

12 11 10 09 08 07 06 05   5 4 3 2 1

ISBN 0-7847-1786-9

Table of Contents

• New Testament Crafts

• Seasonal Crafts

Introduction

The following pages contain over 100 Bible crafts, plus an extra section of holiday and seasonal crafts! These crafts were designed especially for children ages 6-8. Each craft is divided into sections to make it easy for you to use.

WHAT YOU NEED

lists all the materials you will need to gather for the craft.

WHAT YOU PREPARE

lists step-by-step simple instructions for preparing the craft.

WHAT YOU DO

lists numbered, step-by-step simple instructions for completing the craft with the children.

WHAT YOU TALK ABOUT

lists two or three simple conversation starters that relate the craft to the Bible story.

WANT TO DO MORE?

is an optional section that contains rhymes, songs, or extra suggestions for the craft.

HOW TO FIND CRAFTS

The crafts are arranged in biblical order. Look in the Table of Contents to find a particular Scripture or story. If you are searching for a particular type of craft, look in the index on pages 156, 157. If you are using HeartShaper™ Preschool/Pre-K & K curriculum, look on pages 158, 159 to find the crafts that correlate with each Bible story.

PARENTS' PAGE

The Parents' Page on pages 7 and 8 is provided to aid you in collecting materials for the crafts. The items are listed in alphabetical order to make it easier for you to check them off once they've been collected.

Parents' Page

We've got some wonderful and fun projects in store for your children as we teach them about God and His love! If you can assist us by donating the following marked items, your help would be greatly appreciated. Please bring the items to your child's classroom by_____.
Many thanks from your child's teaching staff!

- ❏ 1/2 gallon cardboard juice boxes
- ❏ 10" paper plates
- ❏ 12" chenille wire
- ❏ 12" yellow paper plates
- ❏ 1-gallon plastic bags with twist ties
- ❏ 20-ounce paper bowls
- ❏ 3" wide fabric flowers
- ❏ 4" x 7" envelopes
- ❏ 7" paper plates decorated with Christmas design
- ❏ 8" white or gold doilies
- ❏ 9" paper plates
- ❏ 9-ounce green paper or plastic cups
- ❏ Adhesive covering in bright colors
- ❏ Aluminum foil
- ❏ Artificial greenery
- ❏ Balloons
- ❏ Bars of soap
- ❏ Bird seed
- ❏ Blue cellophane
- ❏ Blue food coloring
- ❏ Business-sized envelopes
- ❏ Butcher paper
- ❏ Cereal boxes
- ❏ Cinnamon sticks
- ❏ O-shaped cereal
- ❏ Clear adhesive covering
- ❏ Clear or blue hair gel
- ❏ Clear plastic containers from baked goods
- ❏ Clear plastic report covers
- ❏ Coffee filters

- ❏ Colorful cotton crew socks
- ❏ Cotton balls
- ❏ Craft foam
- ❏ Craft glue
- ❏ Craft sticks/jumbo craft sticks
- ❏ Curling ribbon
- ❏ Cylinder-shaped cardboard containers from chips or nuts
- ❏ Dried pineapple or apricot chunks
- ❏ Dry cereal
- ❏ Egg cartons
- ❏ Empty aluminum soda cans
- ❏ Empty, square tissue boxes with top opening
- ❏ Fabric
- ❏ Feathers
- ❏ Felt
- ❏ Fish crackers
- ❏ Flat buttons
- ❏ Flat quilt batting
- ❏ Frozen dinner rolls
- ❏ Fruit-flavored gummed candy
- ❏ Fruit-flavored O-shaped cereal
- ❏ Fruit-flavored puffed cereal
- ❏ Get well cards
- ❏ Gift bows
- ❏ Gift tags
- ❏ Gift wrap
- ❏ Glitter paint or glitter
- ❏ Gummed candy such as worms or fishing type toys

Parents' Page

- ❑ Hard candy at least 1" in size
- ❑ Hard candy smaller than 1", such as peppermints
- ❑ Index cards
- ❑ Individually-wrapped packets of herb tea
- ❑ Individually-wrapped crackers
- ❑ Individually-wrapped small candy bars
- ❑ Individual-sized plastic water bottles, empty
- ❑ Lace ribbon
- ❑ Large cylinder cardboard box such as from oatmeal
- ❑ Large paper clips
- ❑ Large plastic googly eyes
- ❑ Lightweight cardboard such as file folders
- ❑ Lollipops
- ❑ Long cardboard tubes such as from paper towel rolls
- ❑ Lunch-sized paper bags in solid colors
- ❑ Magazines with nature pictures, food pictures, or pictures of children
- ❑ Magnetic strips
- ❑ Marshmallows
- ❑ Masking tape
- ❑ Nativity cards, may be used
- ❑ New pencils or pens
- ❑ Newspaper
- ❑ Old sheets
- ❑ Paper cups: 9-ounce, 7-ounce, 3-ounce
- ❑ Paper napkins
- ❑ Paper plates
- ❑ Photograph of your child
- ❑ Ping Pong balls or plastic golf balls
- ❑ Plaster of paris
- ❑ Plastic drinking straws
- ❑ Plastic eggs
- ❑ Plastic grass
- ❑ Plastic gallon milk or orange juice jugs
- ❑ Plastic light switch covers
- ❑ Plastic liter soda bottles
- ❑ Plastic margarine lids
- ❑ Plastic spoons
- ❑ Pony beads
- ❑ Postage stamps
- ❑ Poster board
- ❑ Resealable sandwich bags
- ❑ Rolls of paper towels
- ❑ Sand or fish tank gravel
- ❑ Sandpaper
- ❑ Short cardboard tubes such as from toilet paper
- ❑ Small boxes such as from crackers or pudding
- ❑ Small jingle bells
- ❑ Small plastic containers with lids such as yogurt cups
- ❑ Small, individually wrapped candy
- ❑ Spring-type clothespins
- ❑ Star stickers
- ❑ Stickers of birds
- ❑ Stickers with a Bible theme
- ❑ Strawberry baskets
- ❑ Streamers
- ❑ 1"-wide fabric ribbon
- ❑ Tissue paper
- ❑ Unbreakable ornaments
- ❑ Uncooked rice or beans
- ❑ Waxed paper
- ❑ Wide clear tape
- ❑ Women's knee-high stockings or pantyhose
- ❑ Wooden rulers or yardsticks
- ❑ Yarn
- ❑ Yellow or blue foam meat trays

Underwater Scene

God Makes the World (Genesis 1)

WHAT YOU NEED
pattern on p. 129
resealable sandwich bags
  (1 per child)
6"x 8" foam meat tray (1 per child)
yellow or blue foam meat trays
hair gel
blue food coloring
wide clear tape
spoon
scissors
crayons
glue

WHAT YOU PREPARE
Duplicate the pattern, one per child.

Before class, prepare the "water" for each child. Scoop about 1/4 cup of hair gel into the zipper bag. Add a drop of blue food coloring if the gel is clear.

Cut two small fish from the yellow foam tray and place in the bag. Carefully close the bag, squeezing out the air.

Fold the zipper over about 1" and tape securely across the top.

WHAT YOU DO
1. Give each child a copy of the duplicated pattern. Have the children color the pictures and cut them out.

2. Glue the pictures to the bottom of the foam meat tray, trimming to fit if needed.

3. Tape the top and bottom of the prepared "water" bag over the ocean scene of the picture.

4. Encourage the children to press gently on the bag to watch the fish swim around.

WHAT YOU TALK ABOUT
Who made the earth and everything in it?
How can we show God our thankfulness by taking
  care of the earth?

WANT TO DO MORE?
Use water instead of hair gel to put in the bag. Add blue food coloring. Add glitter and tiny beads to the water. Tape securely closed.

Animal Hook-up Game

God Makes the Animals (Genesis 1)

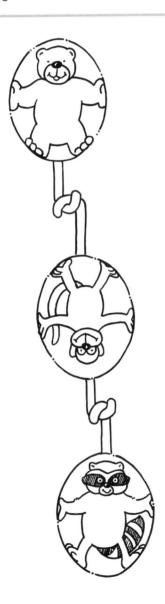

WHAT YOU NEED
animals on p. 130
chenille wire, 6" or 12" lengths
crayons
scissors
glue

WHAT YOU PREPARE
Duplicate two sets of animal patterns for each child. Cut out all the pictures of the animals. Cut the chenille wire into 6" lengths.

WHAT YOU DO

1. Give each child two pictures of each animal. Have the children color the animals.

2. Help the children spread glue on the backs of two matching animal pictures. Place a chenille wire horizontally across the center and sandwich it between the two pictures, gluing in place. Repeat this process to make all six animals.

3. After the glue has dried, bend each end of the chenille wire into a hook.

4. Give the children time to play with their animals, hooking them end to end. They can try to hold one animal and try to hook on all the rest.

WHAT YOU TALK ABOUT
Who made all the animals?
What is your favorite animal?
Why are you thankful God made that animal?

Making Me

God Makes People (Genesis 1)

WHAT YOU NEED
11" x 18" construction paper
poster board
yarn for hair
trims such as buttons, lace, fabric,
    and ribbons
scissors
crayons
glue

WHAT YOU PREPARE
For each child, cut two pieces of 11" x 18" paper in half lengthwise to make four pieces.

Use the illustration below to help you cut simple hands, feet, and faces out of construction paper. All pieces should be approximately eight inches across. If you wish, cut hats for boys and hair bows for girls out of construction paper. If you want the children to cut these out during class, use poster board to make patterns for them to trace.

WHAT YOU DO

1. Let each child choose one color of 11" x 18" paper for the shirt/body and four matching pieces of 5 1/2" x 18" paper for the arms and legs.

2. Help the children fold the arms and legs back and forth with accordion-style folds. Glue the hands and feet to one end of each arm and leg.

3. Color the face. Glue the face, arms, and legs to the shirt/body as shown.

4. Glue yarn on for hair. Let the children glue on accessories such as buttons, lace, hair bows, or caps.

WHAT YOU TALK ABOUT
Who made people?
Why are people so special to God?
How can we show God that He is special to us?

WANT TO DO MORE?
To add more fun to this project, cut out simple skirts and shorts from fabric. The children can glue these on their projects. If you have a blank wall in your classroom, you can tape these to the wall when they are dry. Children may write their names on one of the shoes. This helps them feel like they are important members of the class.

Noah's Ark and Puppets

Noah Obeys God (Genesis 6, 7)

WHAT YOU NEED
animals and ark door on p. 131
egg cartons
craft sticks
11" x 18" brown or tan
    construction paper
crayons
scissors
stapler
glue

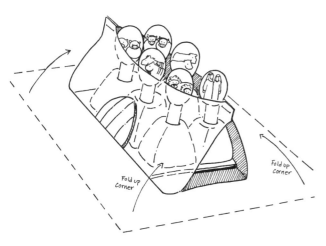

Fold up Corner

Fold up corner

WANT TO DO MORE?
Listen to worship music as you march around the room in a line of pairs. Let each pair of children choose to act out a particular animal as they march. Finish by sitting on a large sheet or rug representing the ark. Say sentence prayers thanking God for keeping His promises.

WHAT YOU PREPARE
Duplicate the animals and ark door, one set for each child.

Cut the egg cartons so there are six dividers sticking up for each child's carton in two rows of three.

Poke a small hole in the top of each point so that there are six holes.

Cut the paper to be 12" long. Fold it into thirds so that the two ends fold into the middle.

WHAT YOU DO
1. Give each child the animals and ark door to color. Have them cut out each picture.

2. Glue each animal picture to a craft stick to make a puppet.

3. Help the children glue their egg cartons on the center of the paper. Fold up the sides and staple each top corner of the sides to form the ark. Glue the door on the front center of the ark.

4. Tell the story of Noah while the children use their puppets to act out the story. Have them move the puppets to the ark and stand each one in its own hole.

WHAT YOU TALK ABOUT
What did God tell Noah to do?
Did Noah obey God?
How can you obey God?

Rainbow Windsock

God Keeps His Promise to Noah (Genesis 8, 9)

WHAT YOU NEED

11" x 18" construction paper
streamers in rainbow colors
yarn, cut into 3' lengths
hole punch
scissors
glue
clear tape

WHAT YOU PREPARE

Cut seven 12" streamers for each child.

WHAT YOU DO

1. Give each child a piece of construction paper.

2. Help the children glue the streamers along one of the longer edges of the paper.

3. Help the children fold down a 1" fold along the other long edge of the paper.

4. Make a cylinder of the paper, gluing the edges together. Tape if needed.

5. Punch two holes on opposite sides of the top fold of the windsock and tie on a piece of yarn for hanging.

WHAT YOU TALK ABOUT

What did God put in the sky after He kept His promise to Noah?

What can we remember when we see a rainbow?

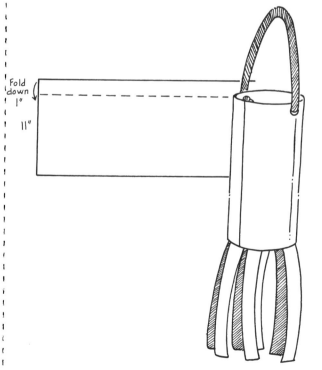

Fold down 1"

11"

WANT TO DO MORE?

Instead of using streamers to make the windsock, use colorful ties instead. Sandwich them between two sheets of paper and staple them securely around the paper cylinder.

Abraham's Map

Abraham's New Home (Genesis 12, 13)

WHAT YOU NEED
Bible
pictures on p. 132
11" x 18" construction paper
black construction paper
crayons
scissors
glue

WHAT YOU PREPARE
Duplicate the pictures, one set per child.

Cut the black paper into 1 1/2" x 12" strips.

Cut four 1 1/2" x 6" strips of paper for each child, any color.

Cut a variety of wide triangles to represent Abraham's tents.

WHAT YOU DO
1. Give each child a piece of large construction paper. Show the children how to glue several strips of black on the construction paper to represent roads.

2. Encourage the children to glue several triangles to the picture to look like Abraham's tents.

3. To make the figures, color the pictures of Abraham and his family. Fold the 6" strips in half and glue one picture to each strip with the top of the picture at the fold. Bend each end of the strip towards the center and glue the ends together. Follow the illustration as a guide.

4. Let the children move the figures around on the map as you retell the story.

WHAT YOU TALK ABOUT
Even though Abraham moved away from his old home, who was always with him?
Who promises to be with us always?

WANT TO DO MORE?
Bring in small plastic toy farm animals to give to the children to keep and use as they play with their story map. Let them take turns telling the story as they move the figures around on the map.

Soccer Game

Abraham Lets Lot Choose First (Genesis 13)

WHAT YOU NEED
label on p. 132
2-liter bottle, 1 per child
ping pong ball, plastic golf ball, or
    typing paper, 1 per child
masking tape
crayons
scissors
craft glue

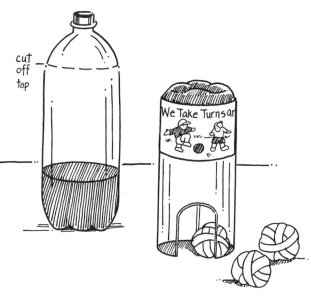

WANT TO DO MORE?
During snack time, let half the children serve
the other half first with crackers or pretzels.
Then switch and have the second group serve
the first with cups of juice.

WHAT YOU PREPARE
Duplicate the label, one per child.

Cut the tops off the plastic bottles.

Cut a semicircle opening from the edge of the
bottle as shown in the illustration.

WHAT YOU DO
1. Have the children color the pictures, cut them out,
and glue them to the bottle. Make sure that the pictures aren't upsidedown. The bottle's bottom should
be at the top of the picture.

2. Give each child a ball. If you're not using balls, give
everyone a sheet of typing paper and demonstrate
how to crumple it up into a paper ball that will fit
through the opening of their bottles. Help the
children wrap their paper balls with 3" lengths of
masking tape to make them sturdy.

3. Divide the children into pairs. Have them stand their
bottles on the floor beside their partner's and try
to kick their balls into the bottles to score a goal. As
they play together, encourage the children to let
each other go first.

WHAT YOU TALK ABOUT
Why did it please God when Abraham let Lot
    choose first?
What are some other times we can choose to do
    right by letting someone else go first?

Happy Hat

The Birth of Isaac (Genesis 15, 17, 18, 21)

WHAT YOU NEED
20-ounce paper bowl, 1 per child
9" paper plate, 1 per child
trims such as ribbons, streamers,
    balloons, chenille wire
stickers
hole punch
stapler
scissors
glue
clear tape

WANT TO DO MORE?
Have a "happy party" where everyone
wears their hats and eats a special snack.
Encourage the children to share about
how God makes them happy. Conclude by
saying a prayer thanking God for keeping
His promises.

WHAT YOU PREPARE
Cut the center out of the paper plate.

To form the hat, staple the bowl to the rim of the
paper plate with four staples. Be sure to keep the
sharp ends of the staples pointing up toward the
top edge of the hat.

Punch holes evenly spaced around the rim of the hat.

Blow the balloons up slightly and knot them.

WHAT YOU DO
1. Encourage the children to decorate their hats by
choosing the trims they like. The knot of the balloons can simply be pulled through the holes to
make them stay.

2. Help the children tie things through the holes
around the rim of the hat. Glue and tape other
decorations around the top of the hat.

WHAT YOU TALK ABOUT
How did God keep His promise to Abraham and Sarah?
How did they feel when God kept His promise?
How does it make you feel to know God keeps
    His promises?

staple
to
plate

Cup of Kindness

Rebekah Is Kind (Genesis 24)

WHAT YOU NEED
gift wrap in a variety of colors
ruler
scissors
clear tape
dry cereal
sandwich-sized plastic bags

WHAT YOU PREPARE
Cut the gift wrap into 10" squares.

WHAT YOU DO

1. Give each child a square of gift wrap. Have them place their squares on the table with the decorated side facing down.

2. Help them fold the squares in half to form a large triangle.

3. Use the illustration as a guide to fold one corner of the triangle over to the side. Then fold the opposite corner of the triangle over to the other side.

4. Fold the front flap of the triangle down over the front. Fold the back flap of the triangle down over the back. Tape if necessary.

5. Let the children each fill a bag with dry cereal. Tape closed. Place their bags of cereal in their cups. Encourage the children to give the cereal as an act of kindness to someone they know.

WHAT YOU TALK ABOUT
How did Rebekah choose to do what was right? How can we be kind to other people?

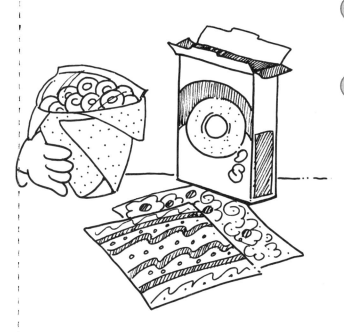

Traffic Sign

Isaac Is a Peacemaker (Genesis 26)

WHAT YOU NEED

8 1/2" x 11" construction paper
white paper
white crayon
red and green paint
paint brushes
scissors
glue

WHAT YOU PREPARE

Cut 5" circles from the white paper. With a white crayon, write "GO" in big letters on the circles.

Cut 5" hexagons from the white paper. With a white crayon, write "STOP" in big letters on the hexagons.

WHAT YOU DO

1. Set up two painting centers for the children. At one center, place red paint out for the children to use. Put the hexagons on the table so that the side that is written on is facing up. Have the children paint the hexagon red. Watch the word "STOP" appear!

2. At the other center, place green paint out for the children to use. Put the circles on the table so that the side that is written on is facing up. Have the children paint the circle green. Watch the word "GO" appear!

3. Let the paintings dry slightly and then glue them to a sheet of construction paper.

WHAT YOU TALK ABOUT

What did Isaac do when he chose to do the right thing?
When will you choose right?
Who helps you do right?

Jacob's Game

God Cares for Jacob (Genesis 28–33)

WHAT YOU NEED
pattern on p. 133
instructions below
index cards (17 per child)
envelopes
crayons
scissors
glue

1. Shuffle the cards.
2. Pass the cards out to the players.
3. Say "Pass." Everyone passes one card to the player on his left.
4. Say "Pass" again. Continue passing cards in this way.
5. When someone's cards match, he should quietly put his finger on his nose. Everyone else should also put a finger on his nose. The last person to put his finger on his nose loses.
6. Play the gane several times.

WHAT YOU PREPARE
Duplicate four sets of pictures and one set of instructions for each child.

If your class has younger children who can't cut very well, cut out all the pictures.

Prepare several sets of cards to use during class.

WHAT YOU DO
1. Give each child four sets of each picture and one instruction sheet. Have the children color the pictures. Glue each picture to an index card.

2. After the cards are dry, put each child's set inside an envelope to keep them from getting lost.

3. Divide the children into groups of four children and help them play the game together several times. Use the classroom sets of cards.

WHAT YOU TALK ABOUT
How did God keep His promise to care for Jacob? How does God take care of you?

Snack Plate

Joseph Does His Best (Genesis 37, 39)

WHAT YOU NEED

sliced cheese
cookie cutters
crackers
small paper plates
1 gallon bags with twist ties

WHAT YOU DO

1. Have the children wash their hands.

2. Encourage the children to do their best work by carefully cutting several shapes from the slices of cheese with the cookie cutters.

3. Arrange the crackers and cheese shapes on the plates. Put each plate in a plastic bag and close.

WHAT YOU TALK ABOUT

When did Joseph do his best work?
How will you do your best work?
Share your snack plate with a friend and remember how Joseph fed many hungry people when he did his best work.

Forgiveness Lollipop

Joseph Forgives His Brothers (Genesis 41–43, 45)

WHAT YOU NEED
pattern on p. 134
lollipop (1 per child)
curling ribbon (optional)
crayons
scissors
glue sticks
clear tape

WHAT YOU PREPARE
Duplicate the pattern, one per child.

WHAT YOU DO

1. Give each child a copy of the picture. Have them color the picture and cut it out. Help the children fold the picture in half and glue the sides together.

2. Place a lollipop inside the paper. Tape the bottom edges of the paper so the lollipop doesn't slip out. Tie on curling ribbon if desired.

3. Encourage the children to keep the lollipop until there is a time they need to ask forgiveness or forgive someone. Give the lollipop as a gift at this time.

WHAT YOU TALK ABOUT
Who did Joseph forgive?
Who do you need to forgive?
How will you show that person that you forgive them?

Baby Moses Basket

God Cares for Moses (Exodus 1, 2)

WHAT YOU NEED
baby Moses from p. 131
strawberry basket, 1 per child
white paper
cotton balls
cotton fabric
crayons
scissors
glue

WHAT YOU PREPARE
Duplicate the baby Moses pattern, one per child.
Cut the fabric into 3" squares, one per child.

WHAT YOU DO

1. Give each child a copy of the picture to color. Have them cut out the picture. Help them trace this onto white paper and cut out a matching shape for the back of the baby Moses.

2. On the center of the back of the baby Moses, glue one jumbo cotton ball or two small cotton balls. Glue the picture of baby Moses to the back, pressing the edges together all around.

3. Glue a square of fabric on top of Moses for his blanket. Place the baby in the basket.

WHAT YOU TALK ABOUT
How did God take care of baby Moses?
How does God take care of us?

God Cares Clock

God Cares for His People (Exodus 7–13)

WHAT YOU NEED
clock on p.135
10" paper plates
plastic margarine lids
paper fasteners
hole punch
crayons
scissors
glue

WANT TO DO MORE?
Let children volunteer to move the arrow on their clocks to a certain time of day and then act out that activity for the other children to see. After each small skit, say a prayer thanking God for caring for us during that time.

WHAT YOU PREPARE
Duplicate the clock, one per child.

Cut a 1" x 3" arrow from the plastic. This will be used for the hand of the clock.

Punch a hole at one end of the arrow.

WHAT YOU DO
1. Give each child a picture of the clock to color and cut out. If you have time, encourage them to draw pictures of things they do throughout the day in the blank circles on the clock.

2. Help the children glue the clocks to the front of the plates.

3. Poke a hole in the center of each clock. Use a paper fastener to mount the plastic hand on each clock as shown.

4. Spend time with the children moving the hand of the clock to the different pictures. As you discuss the meaning of each picture, ask how God cares for us during that time of day.

WHAT YOU TALK ABOUT
How does God take care of you when you are awake?
How does God take care of you when you are asleep?

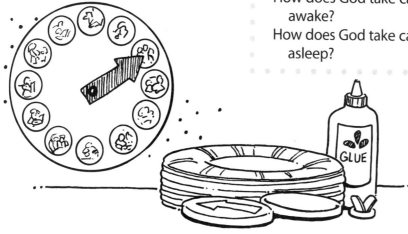

Tambourine

God's People Cross the Red Sea (Exodus 14)

WHAT YOU NEED
10" paper plate (1 per child)
chenille wire, 6" long
small jingle bells
various decorative stickers
crayons
scissors
hole punch

WHAT YOU PREPARE
Cut the center out of each paper plate and discard the center.

Use the hole punch to punch two holes opposite each other in the rim of the plate.

WHAT YOU DO
1. Give each child a paper plate rim to decorate with stickers and crayons.

2. Help the children attach two jingle bells to their tambourines. Thread a chenille wire through one jingle bell and through one of the small holes on the tambourine. Twist the chenille wire in place. Add the second bell through the opposite hole.

WHAT YOU TALK ABOUT
How did God's people thank Him for taking care of them?
How can we thank God for taking care of us?

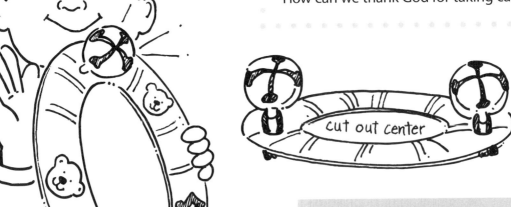

cut out center

WANT TO DO MORE?
Listen to worship music and encourage the children to dance with their tambourines as they join together in praising God.

Pizza Puzzle

God Gives Food and Water (Exodus 16, 17; Numbers 11)

WHAT YOU NEED

10" paper plate (1 per child)
construction paper in a variety of colors, including red
duplicated copies of Psalm 146:7
small bag or envelope
crayons
scissors
glue

WANT TO DO MORE?

Have a pizza party to celebrate how God gives us food. When you're done eating, make several pizza puzzles to keep in the classroom. To make the pizzas, use the large cardboard circles that the pizzas are served on. Let several children decorate each pizza. Cut the pizza into slices. Store the completed puzzle in the actual pizza box.

WHAT YOU PREPARE

Write "God gives food to the hungry. Psalm 146:7" and draw a 6" circle around the verse.

Duplicate this Scripture, one per child. Cut out the circles containing the Scripture.

Cut the red paper into 6" circles.

Cut a variety of pizza toppings shapes from different colors of construction paper such as mushroom, tomato, pepperoni, green pepper, and onion.

WHAT YOU DO

1. Give each child a paper plate, a Scripture verse, and a red circle.

2. Instruct the children to glue the red "sauce" to the front of the plate and the Scripture verse to the back of the plate.

3. Let the children choose how they want to decorate their pizzas. Have them glue the different toppings of their choice on top of the red "sauce."

4. Let the pizzas dry. Cut the pizzas into four or six pieces to resemble pizza slices. Put the slices into a bag or envelope to help carry them home.

WHAT YOU TALK ABOUT

What kind of food does God give to you?
How can you say thank-you to God for the food that you eat?

Scripture Cards

God Gives Ten Rules (Exodus 19, 20, 24, 32)

WHAT YOU NEED
cards on p.136
3" x 5" index cards (10 per child)
small box such as a cracker box,
 about 5 1/2" wide, 1 per child
various decorative stickers
gift wrap
crayons
scissors
glue

WHAT YOU PREPARE
Duplicate the cards, one set per child.

Use the illustration as a guide to cut the top off each small box so that it resembles a business card holder. The front should be about 1" high and the back should be about 3" high.

If the children will be decorating the boxes, cut pieces of gift wrap that fit each side of the box. (Tip: If using boxes of different sizes, keep track of which gift wrap is cut to fit which box by clipping the gift wrap to its corresponding box with a paper clip.)

WHAT YOU DO

1. Give each child a picture of the Scripture verses to color and cut out. Help the children glue each Scripture verse to a separate index card. Decorate with stickers.

2. Glue the pieces of gift wrap to the front, back, and sides of the box.

3. Store the Scripture cards in the holder.

WHAT YOU TALK ABOUT
What rules does your family have that help you? How do God's rules help us?

WANT TO DO MORE?
As you study different Scriptures throughout the year, copy them down on paper, duplicate them, and let the children glue them to index cards. Encourage the children to take the Scripture cards home and display them in the boxes. Set up a memorization chart where the children can put a sticker next to the verses they memorize.

Spyglasses

Joshua and Caleb Believe God (Numbers 13, 14)

WHAT YOU NEED
spyglasses on p. 134
tagboard or heavy paper
chenille wire, 12"
hole punch
crayons
scissors

WHAT YOU PREPARE
Duplicate the glasses pattern on tagboard or heavy paper. Or you can trace the pattern onto tagboard, drawing in the details.

Use the hole punch to punch out one hole at each side of the glasses and two holes for the pupils.

WHAT YOU DO
1 Give each child a set of spyglasses to color.

2 Put a piece of chenille wire at each temple of the glasses, twisting in place. Help the children try on the glasses, bending the wire behind their ears and trimming to fit.

3 Let the children wear their spyglasses as you tell the story.

WHAT YOU TALK ABOUT
How did Joshua and Caleb show that they believed God?
What are some things God wants you to believe?

Marching Puppet

God Is with Moses and Joshua (Deuteronomy 31, 34; Joshua 1)

WHAT YOU NEED
pattern on p. 137
10" paper plate (1 per child)
crayons
scissors
glue

WHAT YOU PREPARE
Cut two 1" holes on the rim of the plate as shown. The children will poke two fingers through these holes. Duplicate the pattern for each child.

WHAT YOU DO
1. Give each child a picture of Joshua to color and cut out.

2. Help the children glue the pictures of Joshua to the plate, following the illustration as a guide. The holes should be where Joshua's legs would be.

3. Show the children how to put their pointer fingers and middle fingers through the holes and march the Joshua puppet around on the table as you tell the story.

WHAT YOU TALK ABOUT
Why were the people afraid to obey God?
Tell about a time when you were afraid to do the right thing.

Wall Puzzle

Joshua Obeys God at Jericho (Joshua 5, 6)

WHAT YOU NEED
pattern from p. 138
cardboard or tagboard
envelope or bag
crayons
scissors
glue

WHAT YOU PREPARE
Duplicate the pattern for each child.

Cut the cardboard into 6 1/2" x 9 1/2" pieces, one per child.

WHAT YOU DO

1. Give each child a picture to color and cut out. Help the children glue the pictures of Jericho's wall to the cardboard.

2. After the picture has dried slightly, cut the puzzle along the dotted lines to have four puzzle pieces.

3. Practice putting the puzzle together and building up the wall. Then mix up the pieces to watch the wall fall down. Place the puzzle pieces in a bag or envelope to carry home.

WHAT YOU TALK ABOUT
How did God's people obey at Jericho?
How can you obey God?

WANT TO DO MORE?
If your classroom has blocks, bring them out for play after this lesson. Practice building the wall of Jericho and then push it down.

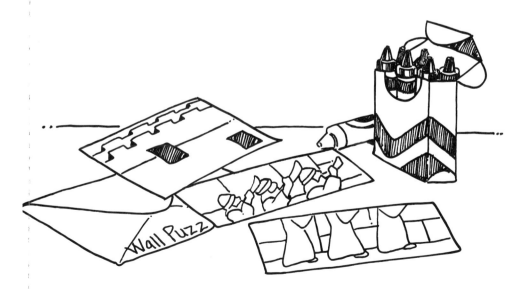

House of Obedience

God's People Choose to Serve Him (Joshua 24)

WHAT YOU NEED

house from p. 139 and pictures
   from p. 137
empty cereal box (1 per child)
construction paper
crayons
scissors
clear wide tape
glue

WHAT YOU PREPARE

Tape the cereal box closed.

Duplicate the house and pictures for each child.

Cut the door and the windows along the dotted
lines, folding them back as flaps.

WHAT YOU DO

1. Give each child a set of pictures to color and cut out.
Then give each child an empty cereal box.

2. Help the children glue a piece of construction paper
to the front of the box of cereal. Have them glue
the picture of the house over the construction paper,
being careful not to glue down the door or windows.
Trim the sides of the construction paper and the
house to better fit the box, if needed.

3. Let the children choose which pictures they want
to glue behind each window and door. Glue these
pictures in place.

WHAT YOU TALK ABOUT

How did God's people do right?
How are the people in your house choosing to do
   the right things?

WANT TO DO MORE?

Instead of using cereal boxes, you may glue the
pictures of the houses onto construction paper.
The children can then draw the members of their
families playing outside the house or doing things
to obey God.

My Story Book

Deborah Helps Barak Obey (Judges 4)

WHAT YOU NEED
book on p. 140
crayons

WHAT YOU PREPARE
Duplicate the book for each child.

WHAT YOU DO

1 Give each child a copy of the book to color. Show the children how to fold the paper to make the book.

2 Read the book together, explaining what happened in each picture. Let the children take turns reading their books to the class.

WHAT YOU TALK ABOUT
How can your friend help you do something when you don't really want to do it?
How can you help your friend do the right thing?

Banner of Bravery

Gideon Is Brave (Judges 6, 7)

WHAT YOU NEED
pattern on p. 141
8 1/2" x 11" construction paper
yarn
hole punch
crayons
scissors
glue

WHAT YOU PREPARE
Duplicate the pattern for each child.

Fold down a 1" flap along the shorter edge of a piece of construction paper, one per child. Glue in place.

Punch two holes on the fold at opposite edges as shown in the illustration.

On each banner, tie on a 2' piece of yarn as a hanger.

WHAT YOU DO
1. Give each child the banner of construction paper.

2. Give each child a picture to color and cut out.

3. Help the children glue the words in the correct order on the banner as shown.

WHAT YOU TALK ABOUT
Why was it hard for Gideon to fight such a big army?
Do you ever feel too little to do something you know you're supposed to do?
Who will help you be brave enough to do the right thing?

Tie in back

God is with you!

JUDGES 6:12

GLUE

WANT TO DO MORE?
Use the banners to decorate the church. You can also make special banners by using fabric or felt as the background instead of paper. Put a dowel rod through the fold at the top to help the banner hang straight. Try making a large banner from fabric to decorate the church. You can glue on large felt letters. The children can put painted handprints all over the banner to show that they want to be brave and do the right thing.

Flower Necklace

Ruth Works Hard (Ruth 1, 2)

WHAT YOU NEED
pictures of flowers, 1-2",
   (found in magazines, garden
   catalogs, and on gift wrap)
white paper
clear adhesive covering
yarn
hole punch
scissors
glue

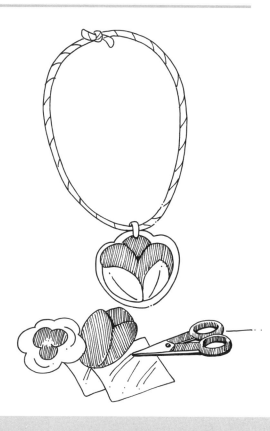

WHAT YOU PREPARE
Cut out a variety of flower pictures, making sure they're smaller than 2" wide.

Cut the adhesive-backed paper into 3" squares. It takes two squares to make one necklace.

Cut the yarn into 3' lengths.

WHAT YOU DO

1 Let the children choose which flower they want to use to make a necklace. Have them glue the flower picture to a piece of white paper. Cut the flower out.

2 Help the children peel off the paper from one adhesive-backed square. Show them how to carefully place the flower in the center of the square. Peel off the paper from a second square and place it over the first so that the flower is sandwiched in the middle.

3 Cut around the flower, leaving an edge of clear plastic all around the flower.

4 Use the hole punch to punch a hole at the top of the flower. Tie on a yarn string to make a necklace. The children may keep the necklaces or give them as gifts.

WHAT YOU TALK ABOUT
How did you feel when you tried to do your best work on this craft?
Tell about another time when you can choose to work hard and do your best.

WANT TO DO MORE?
Have the children bring in real, small flowers the week ahead. Let them help you spread out the flowers on waxed paper. Cover these with another sheet of waxed paper and weight them down with books. Dry one week.

Nesting dolls

Hannah Keeps a Promise (1 Samuel 1)

WHAT YOU NEED
pattern from p. 142
3 paper cups in 3 sizes: 9-ounce,
   7-ounce, and 3-ounce
   (1 set per child)
crayons
scissors
glue
clear tape

WHAT YOU PREPARE
Duplicate the three nesting-doll figures from page 142.

WHAT YOU DO

1 Give each child a set of the three pictures to color and cut out.

2 Give each child a set of cups. Stand the cups upside-down. Help the children glue the pictures to the cups: Eli to the largest cup, Hannah to the middle-sized cup, and Samuel to the smallest cup. Be careful that the cups are standing upside down when you glue on the pictures.

3 Stack the cups from smallest to largest. Tell the story and encourage the children to unstack the cups as you go.

WHAT YOU TALK ABOUT
How did Hannah do the right thing by keeping the promise she made?
What is something you have promised to do at home?
How can you do right and keep your promise?

Samuel's Bed

Samuel Listens and Obeys (1 Samuel 2, 3, 7)

WHAT YOU NEED
pattern on p. 142
construction paper, 12" x 18"
fabric
crayons
scissors
glue stick

WHAT YOU PREPARE
Duplicate the pattern for each child.

Cut the construction paper in four rectangles, each measuring about 6 1/2" x 10".

Cut a 6 1/2" square of fabric for each child.

WHAT YOU DO
1. Give each child a sheet of prepared construction paper, a square of fabric, and a picture of Samuel. Have the children color in Samuel and cut him out.

2. To form the bed and blanket, help the children spread a line of glue close to three edges of the fabric. (Don't spread any glue in the middle of the fabric.) Press the fabric on top of the paper as shown.

3. Slip Samuel into the pocket that is formed. The children may draw a pillow under his head if they want.

WHAT YOU TALK ABOUT
How did Samuel do the right thing?
How can you do the right thing when you're
   playing with your friends?

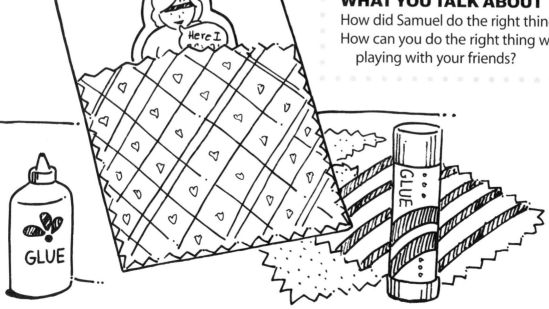

Crown

Samuel Obeys God (1 Samuel 8–10)

WHAT YOU NEED
10" paper plate (1 per child)
hard candy, less than 1" wide, such
   as peppermints
scissors
glue

WHAT YOU PREPARE
Cut the center of each plate to make the points of the crown, being careful not to cut the rim of the plate. Follow the illustration as a guide to cut the plate into eighths.

Fold the points up, crease the fold, and then flatten the plates again.

WHAT YOU DO
1. Give each child a prepared plate.

2. Show the children how to glue a candy or two on each point of the crown. Be careful to place the candy close to the fold (not at the tip top of the point) but not on the fold. Candy may also be glued on the rim of the plate.

3. After the glue is dry, fold up the points of the crown and wear the crown.

WHAT YOU TALK ABOUT
How did Samuel obey when he didn't want
   to obey?
Are there ever times you don't want to obey
   your parents?
What happens when we don't obey our parents?

Heart Pillow

Saul Disobeys God (1 Samuel 15)

WHAT YOU NEED
red or pink roll paper
white paper
tissue paper or shredded newspaper
stapler
pen or marker
glue

WANT TO DO MORE?
Before the pillows are stuffed, the children can decorate their pillows with rubber stamps or decorative stickers. They can glue on bits of lace and buttons.

WHAT YOU PREPARE
Draw a large heart on a piece of white paper. Inside the heart, write "I will obey God's laws with all my heart. Psalm 119:34." Duplicate one of these for each child.

Cut large hearts from the roll paper, 2' to 3' wide. It takes two hearts to make each pillow.

Staple pairs of hearts together around the edges, leaving one side open for stuffing. The opening should be about 10" wide.

WHAT YOU DO
1. Give each child a heart from roll paper and a smaller heart with the verse on it.

2. Let the children color the smaller heart, cut it out, and glue it to the center of the large roll paper heart.

3. Help the children lightly stuff their pillows with tissue or shredded newspaper. Staple the opening closed.

WHAT YOU TALK ABOUT
How did Saul disobey God?
When have you disobeyed God?
How will you choose to obey?

Light Switch Cover

Samuel Anoints David as King (1 Samuel 16)

WHAT YOU NEED

light switch cover from p. 143
plastic light switch covers (1 per
    child, available in hardware
    stores)
craft glue (regular white glue
    doesn't work well)
crayons
scissors

WHAT YOU PREPARE

Duplicate a light switch cover for each child.

WHAT YOU DO

1. Give each child a picture to color and cut out.

2. Help the children cut out the center rectangle of the picture.

3. Have them glue their pictures on the light switch covers, centering the hole over the hole for the light switch.

WHAT YOU TALK ABOUT

Do you feel afraid when it's dark in your bedroom? When you feel afraid, say Psalm 56:3 aloud. Ask God to help you trust in Him.

When I am afraid, I will trust in you.
Psalm 56:3

David's Sheep

David Does His Job (1 Samuel 16, 17)

WHAT YOU NEED
sheep head and ear from p. 130
long cardboard tubes such as from paper towels
flat batting such as is used for making quilts
black construction paper
black marker
spring-type clothespins
waxed paper
scissors
glue

WHAT YOU PREPARE
Cut each tube in half to make two 6" tubes.

Use the marker to color in a 1/2"-wide black band around the bottom edge of each tube.

Use the illustration as a guide to cut out the legs of the sheep so they're about 2" long.

Cut the batting into 3" x 7 1/2" rectangles.

Cut out two ears for each child from black construction paper.

Trace and cut out a sheep's face for each child.

WHAT YOU DO
1. Help each child spread glue on the upper part of the cardboard tube. Wrap the batting around the tube to form the body of the sheep. Hold the edges in place with two clothespins while it dries. (If there is an excess amount of glue under the batting, use waxed paper to protect the clothespins from sticking.)

2. Have the children glue the face and two ears on their sheep.

WHAT YOU TALK ABOUT
What jobs do you do at home? At school?
How will God help you to do your jobs?

Pop-up Puppet

David Is Brave (1 Samuel 17)

WHAT YOU NEED
figures of David and Goliath from
   p. 133
poem from p. 134
small box such as pudding or
   sticks of margarine come in
craft sticks
crayons
scissors
glue

WHAT YOU PREPARE
Duplicate one set of figures and one poem for each child. Cut one end off the box so that it is 3" tall. Cut a 3/4" slit in the bottom of the box.

WHAT YOU DO

1. Have the children color in Goliath, David, and the poem. Cut them out.

2. Show them how to glue the picture of David and the poem on opposite sides of the box. The opening of the box will be at the top.

3. Glue Goliath on a craft stick. Insert the puppet into the top of the box and pull the stick out through the bottom slit.

4. Read the poem aloud. In the beginning, hold Goliath up out of the box. When he falls down, pull him down inside the box.

WHAT YOU TALK ABOUT
How big was Goliath?
Do you think David was scared?
When are some times that you are scared?
Who will help you when you are scared?

WANT TO DO MORE?
Sometimes children face very scary things in their lives. Use this time to pray with them and ask God to help them be brave and to help them with their problems.

Catch and Toss

David and Jonathan Are Friends (1 Samuel 18–20)

WHAT YOU NEED
2 paper bowls for each child
poster board
newspaper
masking tape
stapler
washable markers
various decorative stickers
scissors

WHAT YOU PREPARE
Cut the poster board into 1 1/2" x 10""strips. (Make a finished craft to make sure that these strips are the right length for the size of the bowls you are using. Adjust the length of the strips to fit your bowls.)

WHAT YOU DO
1. Give each child two poster board strips to decorate with markers and stickers. Only decorate one side of each strip.

2. Staple the decorated strips to the bottom of the bowls as shown in the illustration. This forms a strap on the bowls so they can be worn as a catcher's mitt. The straps should have about a 1/2" space so that a child's hand may fit easily into the mitt. Each child will have two mitts.

3. Give the children sheets of newspaper and show them how to crumble them loosely into 5" balls. Use 6" lengths of masking tape to tape around the ball so that it will keep its shape. Each ball will need three to four strips of tape.

4. Allow time for the children to play games of catch with their friends. Encourage them to play at home with their friends by sharing their mitts.

WHAT YOU TALK ABOUT
Who was the friend God gave David?
What friends has God given you?
How do your friends help you?

Gingerbread Boy

David Does the Right Thing (1 Samuel 26)

WHAT YOU NEED

brown construction paper
1/2" flat buttons
spices such as allspice, cloves, and
cinnamon
scissors
crayons
glue

WHAT YOU PREPARE

Using the illustration below as a guide, make two simple gingerbread boy patterns for each child.

If your class has a lot of younger children who can't use scissors very well, cut out the two gingerbread patterns for them.

WHAT YOU DO

1 Give each child two gingerbread boy patterns. Have the children color the gingerbread patterns and cut them out.

2 Help the children spread glue over the inside of the back of the gingerbread boy. Sprinkle spices generously over the glue.

3 Glue the front of the gingerbread boy to the back. Glue on buttons for eyes and decoration.

WHAT YOU TALK ABOUT

What are some ways we can be kind?
Who helps us share, forgive others, and love each other?

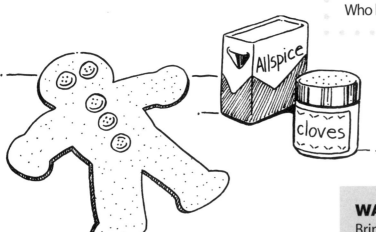

WANT TO DO MORE?

Bring gingerbread cookies to the classroom. Help the children place a couple of cookies on a plate with their gingerbread boy. Encourage the children to be kind and give the plate of cookies to someone they know.

Stained Glass Window

Solomon Prays for Wisdom (1 Kings 3, 4)

WHAT YOU NEED
poster board
aluminum foil
tissue paper, brightly colored
11" x 18" black construction paper
paint brushes
shallow bowls
clear tape
scissors
white glue

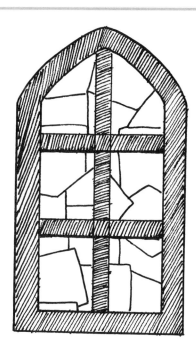

WHAT YOU PREPARE
Cut the poster board into the shape of a stained glass window that is about 10" wide and 17" tall. Cut one window for each child.

Cover one side of each window with a sheet of 20" long aluminum foil, gluing in place. Fold the extra foil to the back of the window and use tape to hold it flat.

Cut the tissue into 2" squares or triangles.

In shallow bowls, make a mixture of 1/2 white glue and 1/2 water.

WHAT YOU DO
1. Show the children how to place the tissue paper shapes on the foil-covered side of the window. Use the paintbrush to paint the glue mixture over the tissue.

2. After the windows are covered with tissue, glue the window to a black piece of construction paper as a frame.

3. Cut two 1" x 11" strips and one 1" x 18" strip of black paper for each window. Help the children glue the strips of black paper to their windows as shown.

WHAT YOU TALK ABOUT
What did Solomon ask God to give him?
What good things can we ask God to give to us?

Raven with Treat

God Cares for Elijah (1 Kings 17)

WHAT YOU NEED
2 dinner-sized paper plates for
    each child
12" chenille wire
black and orange construction
    paper
white or yellow crayons or colored
    pencils
individually wrapped crackers or
    crackers and small plastic bags
    with twist ties
stapler
hole punch
glue

WHAT YOU PREPARE
Use the illustration as a guide to cut about 3" off one side of one of the plates.

Staple the two plates together with the tops of the plates facing each other to form a pocket.

Use the hole punch to punch two holes in the plate as shown.

Cut 3" diamond shapes and 3" legs/feet from the orange paper for the ravens' beaks and legs.

Cut 1" black circles for the eyes.

WHAT YOU DO
1. Help the children trace around both their hands on black construction paper with the white or yellow crayon. Have them cut out the two handprints for the wings of the ravens.

2. Glue the eyes, beak, legs, and wings to the front of the raven as shown. Twist a chenille wire through the holes to form a hanger for the raven.

3. Place a treat of crackers in the pocket of the raven. Encourage the children to hang the ravens up in their kitchen and fill with an occasional treat.

WHAT YOU TALK ABOUT
How did God take care of Elijah? Each time we eat our food, let's take time to pray and thank God for taking care of us.

Power Mix

God Gives Elijah Food (1 Kings 17)

WHAT YOU NEED
large mixing bowls
measuring cups
sandwich-sized resealable bags
fruit-flavored puffed cereal
fruit-flavored O-shaped cereal
fruit-flavored gummed candy
dried pineapple and apricot chunks
raisins

WHAT YOU PREPARE
If the pineapple or apricot pieces are too large, snip them into tiny chunks the size of raisins.

WHAT YOU DO
1. Since the children will be handling food, have them wash their hands with soap. Divide the children into small groups. Each group will have a mixing bowl and a measuring cup.

2. Give each group portions of each ingredient. Encourage the children to take turns scooping the ingredients into the mixing bowl. Use equal amounts of each cereal in the Power Mix. Use about a fourth of that amount of the candy, fruit chunks, and raisins. Mix the ingredients by tossing lightly.

3. Serve the Power Mix for snack time if you choose. Help each child scoop a portion of Power Mix into a small bag to take home.

WHAT YOU TALK ABOUT
How did God take care of Elijah and the widow?
How does God use His power to take care of us?

Tic-tac-toe

God Shows His Power Through Elijah (1 Kings 18)

WHAT YOU NEED
flame and trophy pattern on p. 130
construction paper
thin ribbon
small envelope
ruler
pen
glue sticks
crayons
scissors

WHAT YOU PREPARE
Duplicate enough flames and trophies for each child to have five flames or five trophies.

Cut the construction paper into 8/2" or 9" squares, one square for each child.

Divide the squares into thirds with a ruler and draw a tic-tac-toe grid on each.

Cut four pieces of ribbon for each child that measure the width of each square.

WHAT YOU DO

1 Give each child a square. Show them how to use their glue sticks to draw a line of glue on the grid-lines and glue the four pieces of ribbon down on the square. This forms the tic-tac-toe board.

2 Give each child five flames or five trophies to color and cut out. Take time to show the children how to play tic-tac-toe. Each player will use either the flame or the trophy as the X's and O's.

3 Put the small pieces into an envelope to take home.

WHAT YOU TALK ABOUT
Who is the most powerful in the whole, wide world? Whose power always wins?

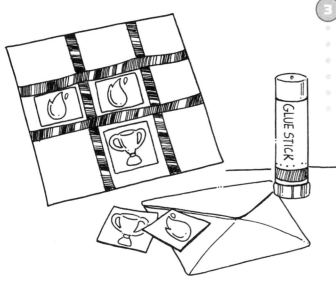

Ring Toss Game

Micaiah Tells the Truth (1 Kings 22)

WHAT YOU NEED

paper
poster board
round plastic lids such as from
    yogurt or sour cream containers
hole punch
yarn
crayons
scissors
glue

Tell
the
Truth

WHAT YOU PREPARE

Use the illustration below as a guide to make a simple Micaiah figure on a piece of paper. The arm on the figure should stick up at least 3", and the total height of the figure should be 9"-10". Duplicate the figure for each child in the class.

Glue the figures on poster board. Cut them out after they dry.

To form the ring, cut the center from the plastic lid, leaving a 3 1/2" edge. The ring should be at least 1/2" in diameter. Make sure the rings will fit on Micaiah's arm.

WHAT YOU DO

1. Give each child the poster board picture of Micaiah to color.

2. Punch a hole as shown and tie on a 2' length of yarn. Tie the other end of the yarn to the ring. The yarn should be about 7"-10" in length. Trim the excess yarn.

3. Show the children how to toss the ring and catch it on Micaiah's hand.

WHAT YOU TALK ABOUT

When did Micaiah tell the truth?
Tell about a time when you told the truth.

Door Hanger

God Brings a Boy Back to Life (2 Kings 4)

WHAT YOU NEED
boy and circle patterns on p. 144
poster board
paper fasteners
hole punch
crayons
scissors
glue

WHAT YOU PREPARE
Duplicate the patterns, one per child.

Glue the pattern to poster board. Cut out both pieces when the glue is dry.

Use the scissors or a pen to poke a hole in the center of the circle.

Use the hole punch to punch a hole in the one eye of the boy.

WHAT YOU DO
1. Give each child a boy and a circle to color.

2. After coloring, help the children assemble the boy as shown.

3. Turn the wheels together and practice reading aloud what the boy is saying.

WHAT YOU TALK ABOUT
How did God show his power to the Shunammite woman?
What good things can you say to describe God?

Turn Wheel

Naaman Puppet

God Heals an Obedient Naaman (2 Kings 5)

WHAT YOU NEED
Naaman body strip and faces strip
   on p. 143
2 toilet paper cardboard tubes for
   each child
crayons
scissors
glue

WANT TO DO MORE?
When the craft is dry, twist the cardboard tube so that Naaman's sad face is at the front of the puppet. Begin telling the story of Naaman. At the part where God heals Naaman, have the children twist the happy faces to be at the front of the puppets. The children may wear the puppets on their fingers.

WHAT YOU PREPARE
Duplicate the two strips, one per child.

Cut one cardboard tube into two pieces so that one piece is 3" long and the other piece is 2" long.

Squeeze the uncut tube and slide the two pieces of the first tube over it. The uncut tube will have a wrinkle in it.

WHAT YOU DO

1. Give each child a copy of the duplicated body and face strips. Have them color the pictures and cut them out.

2. Use the illustration as a guide to show the children how to glue Naaman's faces to the 2" section of the tube.

3. Glue Naaman's body to the 3" section of the tube to form the front of the puppet.

WHAT YOU TALK ABOUT
How did God show His power to Naaman?
How does God show His power to us?

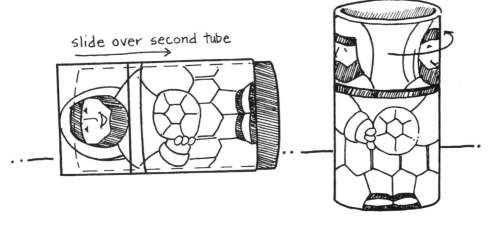

slide over second tube

King Hezekiah Doll

Hezekiah Prays for Healing (2 Kings 20)

WHAT YOU NEED

paper

large, cardboard oatmeal cylinder boxes without the lids (1 per child)

11" x 18" construction paper

crayons

scissors

clear tape

WHAT YOU PREPARE

On the paper, draw a 3 1/4" circle. Using the illustration as a guide, draw Hezekiah's face on the circle. Duplicate the face for each child.

Cut orange or yellow construction paper in half lengthwise, cutting the two halves into two crowns. Cut 1" x 18" strips of paper for belts. Cut 3" circles in half to form pairs of shoes. Prepare a crown, belt, and shoes for each child to use.

WHAT YOU DO

1. Help the children glue a large piece of construction paper around the empty oatmeal box. Tape the edge of the paper if necessary.

2. Spread glue around the bottom edge of the crown and glue it to the top of the oatmeal box as shown.

3. Glue on the face and the belt. Glue on the two shoes.

WHAT YOU TALK ABOUT

When you are sick, whom can you pray to for help to get well?

How did God answer Hezekiah's prayer when the king was sick?

WANT TO DO MORE?

Give each child several Get Well cards to place inside the King Hezekiah doll. Encourage the children to share their dolls with family members who might be sick. Each child can give one of the cards to a sick person and place the doll in the sick person's room. Encourage the children to pray for the sick person. The doll can remind the sick person of their prayers for healing.

Book and Bible Holder

King Josiah Obeys the Law (2 Kings 22, 23)

WHAT YOU NEED
empty cereal box (1 box for every 2 children)

construction paper in a variety of colors

various Christian stickers

scissors

glue

crayons

WHAT YOU PREPARE
Cut each cereal box in half to form two book holders as shown.

WHAT YOU DO

1. Help the children trace the sides of the cereal boxes onto construction paper.

2. Cut out the construction paper. Decorate the paper by drawing pictures and glue it to the sides of the box.

3. Add stickers to the design on the box.

4. Encourage the children to take their Book and Bible Holders home and keep Christian books, CD's, videos, or Bibles in them.

WHAT YOU TALK ABOUT
Who found the book of God's law in our story?

What books do you have at home that tell you about God?

WANT TO DO MORE?
This would be a nice opportunity to give each child a small book that tells about Jesus. Encourage the children to keep their collection of Christian books in a handy spot. Speak to the children's parents about today's lesson and encourage the parents to read a Bible story each day to their children at home.

Shield

Jehoshaphat Prays for Help (2 Chronicles 20)

WHAT YOU NEED
2 large paper plates for each child
yarn
construction paper
decorations such as feathers or
    various stickers
hole punch
clear tape
scissors
crayons
stapler
glue

WHAT YOU PREPARE
Cut a center strip from one paper plate that measures about 2" wide.

Staple this strip to the second paper plate to form the handle of the shield. (Make sure the tops of the plates are facing each other.)

Punch holes about 2" apart, spaced evenly around the plate.

Cut the yarn into 4' lengths. Cover one end with clear tape to form a needle. Tie the other end of the yarn onto the plate, leaving a 4" tail.

WHAT YOU DO
1. Show the children how to lace the yarn around the edge of the shield. Use the 4" tail to tie off the knot. Trim excess.

2. Let the children decorate the fronts of the shields with crayons or by gluing on paper shapes, feathers, and other decorations.

WHAT YOU TALK ABOUT
Who can help us when we are afraid?
How did God help Jehoshaphat when the king
    was afraid?

WANT TO DO MORE?
Ask children to share times that they are afraid. Pray for each child during group prayer time, asking God to help protect them from their fears.

Cleaning Apron

Manasseh Prays for Forgiveness (2 Chronicles 33)

WHAT YOU NEED
paper
paper towels
1"-wide fabric ribbon
8 1/2" x 11" construction paper
crayons
stapler
scissors
glue

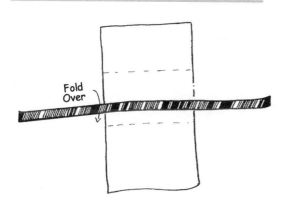

Create in Me a
Pure ♥ O God.
Psalm 51:10

WHAT YOU PREPARE
Tear off the paper towels so that three sheets are connected together. Each child will need four or five sets of these.

Cut the paper into 8 1/2"x 3" strips. Use the illustration as a guide to print the verse (*NIV*) on the strips.

WHAT YOU DO

1 Have the children color the verse and cut it out. Fold a piece of construction paper in half lengthwise and have the children glue the verse so that the top of the verse is near the outside fold as shown.

2 Measure the ribbon around the child's waist, adding about 1' for tying.

3 Assemble the cleaning apron by stacking five layers of paper towels facedown on the table. Place the ribbon across the center of the towels and fold the towels over in half so that the ribbon is sandwiched in between. Place the picture over the folded paper towels, using the illustration as a guide. Staple the picture, towels, and ribbon together with about three staples across the top.

4 Help the children tie the aprons on around their waists.

WHAT YOU TALK ABOUT
When we tell God we're sorry, He forgives us.
He cleans away all the wrong things we've done.
Everyone makes mistakes, even kings.
Who should we talk to if we make a mistake and do something wrong?

WANT TO DO MORE?
Encourage the children to tear off and use one of their paper towels to help clean the classroom. As you are cleaning together, talk about how God makes our hearts clean from wrong things we do.

Happy and Sad Puppet

Ezra and Nehemiah Help the People Do Right (Nehemiah 1, 2, 4, 6, 8)

WHAT YOU NEED
11" x 18" construction paper in a variety of colors including red
scissors
glue sticks

WHAT YOU PREPARE
Cut 6"-wide smiles from red paper.

Cut large ovals, circles, and triangles to use as noses and eyes.

WHAT YOU DO
1. Help each child fold a sheet of paper in half and spread a line of glue along both sides. (Don't glue the bottom of the puppet.)

2. Show the children how to make a smiling face on one side of the puppet and a frowning face on the other side of the puppet by gluing on the paper shapes to form faces.

WHAT YOU TALK ABOUT
How do we feel when we do something right?
How do we feel when we know we've done something wrong?

WANT TO DO MORE?
Seat the children in a group, wearing the puppets over their hands. Describe different situations from the Bible story. If the people did right, have the children hold up the smiling face. If the people did wrong, have them hold up the frowning face. Describe different situations that the children face each day. Encourage them to show either the happy or sad face according to whether the right or wrong choice was made.

Kitchen Banner

Queen Esther Helps Others (Esther 2–5, 7, 8)

WHAT YOU NEED
paper
felt
fabric flowers about 3" wide
   (1 per child)
jumbo craft sticks
12" chenille wire
scissors
craft glue
crayons

WHAT YOU PREPARE
Cut the paper into 2 1/2" x 3" pieces. Using the illustration below as a guide, print the verses onto the pieces of paper.

Cut the felt into 4" x 12" pieces.

Cut the flower stem to be about 4" long.

WHAT YOU DO

1. Give each child the verse paper to color. Use the craft glue to glue the verse to the bottom front of the banner.

2. Snip three parallel 1/2" slits about 3" above the picture. Help the children slide the flower stem through the slits so that the flower is at the front and the stem hangs down behind the banner.

3. Fold over the top 2" of the felt, placing a jumbo craft stick inside the fold. Glue in place.

4. Attach a chenille wire as shown to form a hanger.

WHAT YOU TALK ABOUT
Why was it hard for Queen Esther to do the right thing?
Describe a time when it was hard for you to choose between right and wrong.
Who will give us the strength to do the right thing?

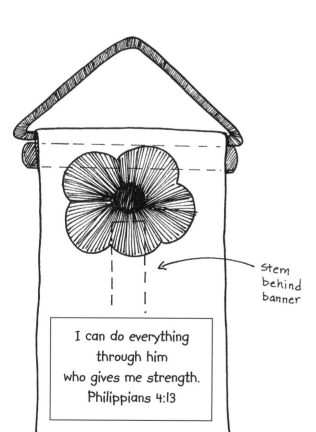

Stem behind banner

I can do everything
through him
who gives me strength.
Philippians 4:13

Note Holder

Job Does What Is Right (Job 1, 2, 42)

WHAT YOU NEED

arms, legs, and face patterns on
    p. 143
dessert-sized paper plate in a solid,
    cheerful color (not plastic plate)
short cardboard tube such as from
    toilet paper (1 per child)
index cards (5 per child)
scissors
crayons
glue

WANT TO DO MORE?

Hold up the index cards and read them carefully to the children, pointing to the words. Then perform small skits that act out different situations in which the children will need to choose right from wrong.

WHAT YOU PREPARE

Duplicate the patterns for each child.

Cut a slit across the middle of the cardboard tube as shown in the illustration.

Write different sentences on the index cards that encourage doing right things. For instance: I will take turns, I will help, I will listen, I will share, I will say "Thank-you," I will say "Please."

WHAT YOU DO

1. Give each child a picture to color and cut out. Help the children glue the arms and legs to the top of the paper plate, making sure that they are spaced closely enough for the cardboard tube to be glued on top.

2. Spread a thin line of glue across the bottom of the cardboard tube (opposite the slit), and use the illustration as a guide to glue the tube to the paper plate.

3. Glue the face to the end of the tube closest to the arms.

4. Let each child choose five index cards. The children can color the cards and place them in the note holder after the glue has dried.

WHAT YOU TALK ABOUT

Who chose right in our story?
Who will help us make the right choices?
What are some right choices you will make?

Healthy Placemat

Daniel and His Friends Eat Good Food (Daniel 1)

WHAT YOU NEED

11" x 18" construction paper in a
  variety of colors
magazine pictures of healthy foods
  (no junk food or candy)
scissors
glue

WANT TO DO MORE?

Encourage the children to use
their placemats at home to
remind them to eat healthy
food. If you laminate the
placemats, they will last longer.

WHAT YOU PREPARE

Use the illustration as a guide to cut some of the
construction paper into large circles for plates,
small circles for cups, triangles for napkins, and
silverware sets.

Cut out pictures from magazines that show
healthy foods.

WHAT YOU DO

1 Let the children choose different paper shapes to
put on their placemat and glue these in place.

2 Give the children time to browse through the magazine pictures to choose foods that they want to
glue on their plates.

WHAT YOU TALK ABOUT

Why does God want us to eat healthy foods?
Was it hard for Daniel and his friends to eat the
  right foods?
Which foods are healthy for our body?

Puppet Theater

Daniel's Friends Face a Fiery Furnace (Daniel 3)

WHAT YOU NEED
2 figures from p. 145
plastic gallon jug such as from milk
   or juice (1 per child)
orange construction paper
craft sticks
crayons
scissors
glue

WANT TO DO MORE?
Retell the story from the Bible as the children act it out with their puppets and stage. You could also let the children make a king puppet and soldier puppets.

WHAT YOU PREPARE
Duplicate the figures for each child.

Cut the front out of the plastic jug as shown to form a furnace puppet stage.

Cut 2" teardrop shapes from orange paper to represent flames of fire in the furnace. Cut about 10 per child.

WHAT YOU DO
1. Give each child a copy of the figures to color and cut out.

2. Glue the two puppets to craft sticks.

3. Glue the flames of fire to the inside of the furnace.

WHAT YOU TALK ABOUT
Was it hard for Daniel's friends to put God first? Describe ways you can put God first.

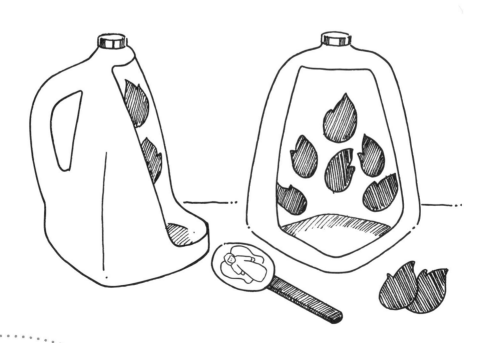

Lion Puppet

Daniel and the Lions' Den (Daniel 6)

WHAT YOU NEED

lion head and teeth patterns on
    p. 145
business-size envelopes
    (1 per child)
crayons
scissors
glue

WHAT YOU PREPARE

Duplicate the patterns for each child.

Prepare the envelope to be used for the puppet by first gluing it closed. Fold it in half, back sides together. On the front, snip away a 3" oval opening for the children to place their fingers.

WHAT YOU DO

1. Give each child a pattern to color and cut out. Show them how to glue the face of the lion to the front of the envelope and the teeth to the inside of the mouth.

2. Demonstrate how to wear the puppet. Let the children wear their puppets as you tell the story. Have them growl when you mention the lions. Have them close their puppets' mouths when the angel protects Daniel through the night.

WHAT YOU TALK ABOUT

Why is it important to talk with God every day?
What can we talk to God about?
God wants to hear about our happy times as well as our sad times.

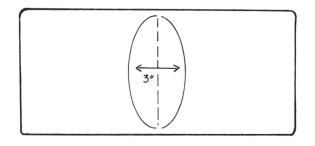

WANT TO DO MORE?

Instead of envelopes, use small boxes such as gelatin boxes to make the lions. Make a slit along the center back and both sides. Fold the two ends of the box forward to resemble how the envelope works. Spray paint the box brown. The children can glue the pattern on the box in a similar manner as they did on the envelope. Add curled ribbon, yarn, or curled paper strips for the lion's mane.

Giant Fish

Jonah Changes His Mind (Jonah 1–3)

WHAT YOU NEED
poster board
permanent marker
crayons
scissors

WHAT YOU PREPARE
Use the illustration as a guide to cut a 12" x 15" fish from the poster board, one per child.

Cut a 4" circle out from the center of the fish.

Use a permanent marker to draw an eye and mouth on the fish.

WHAT YOU DO
1 Give each child a fish to decorate and color.

WHAT YOU TALK ABOUT
Sometimes we make mistakes and disobey.
God wants us to change our minds and choose to obey.
Tell about a time you chose to disobey.
Tell about a time you chose to obey.

WANT TO DO MORE?
Perform a play about Jonah and the fish. When the fish swallows Jonah, the person playing Jonah may peek through the hole in the fish to pretend he is inside.

Shaker Gift

Zechariah Praises God (Luke 1)

WHAT YOU NEED

small box such as a cracker box
   (1 per child)
gift wrap
gift bow (1 per child)
gift tag
uncooked rice or beans
clear tape
pen

WHAT YOU DO

1. Give each child a box. Let the children help scoop about a half-cup of rice or beans into the box. Tape the box closed.

2. Give each child a square of gift wrap to wrap the gift. Tape the bow and the gift tag on the top of the gift. Write the child's name on the gift tag and "FROM: GOD."

WHAT YOU TALK ABOUT

What gift did God give us that John the Baptist was going to tell everyone about?

Why is Jesus' birth the best Christmas gift we can ever get?

WANT TO DO MORE?

Use the shakers during worship time to join in with the music. Praise God for sending John the Baptist to tell everyone about Jesus' birth.

Angel Ornament

An Angel Visits Mary (Luke 1)

WHAT YOU NEED

paper
old sheet music or photocopies of
    sheets of music
8" white or gold doily (1 per child)
yarn in red, green, or white
scissors
crayons
clear tape
glue

WHAT YOU PREPARE

Use the illustration below as a guide to draw a simple angel's face on a circle of paper. Make a face for each child. Cut the sheet music into 6" triangles.

WHAT YOU DO

1. Give each child a picture of the angel's face to color and cut out.

2. Help the children fold the doilies in half and glue together. Glue the triangle of sheet music and the angel's face to the front of the doily as shown.

3. Tape a length of yarn to the back of the ornament for a hanger.

WHAT YOU TALK ABOUT

What important message did the angel tell to Mary? How did Mary feel when she heard the angel's words?

Music Decoration

Mary Sings to God (Luke 1)

WHAT YOU NEED
old sheet music or photocopies of
   old music
red and green curling ribbon
artificial greenery, ornament, or
   cinnamon sticks for each child
   to use
waxed paper
scissors
glue

WHAT YOU PREPARE
Prepare three copies of sheet music for each child.

WHAT YOU DO
1. Help the children spread glue on the backs of the sheet music and roll each sheet into a log.

2. Use a 2' length of curling ribbon to tie the logs together as shown, gluing the logs in place.

3. Let the children choose a piece of decoration to tie on top of the logs. Glue in place.

4. Allow the project to dry on waxed paper or another protected surface.

WHAT YOU TALK ABOUT
Why did Mary sing a worship song to God?
What songs can we sing to worship God?

WANT TO DO MORE?
Sing songs about Jesus' birth during class with your children. When finished, let each child say a simple prayer of thanks to God for sending Jesus as His Son.

Trumpet

Jesus Is Born (Luke 2)

WHAT YOU NEED

paper bowl (1 per child)
12" cardboard tube such as from
    paper towels (1 per child)
plain white paper or 8 1/2" x 11"
construction paper
washable markers
crayons
scissors
glue

WHAT YOU PREPARE

Use the scissors to poke a 1" hole in the center of the bowl. Press the flaps of the hole towards the top of the bowl.

Insert the cardboard tube into the bottom of the bowl about 1/2". Glue the bowl's flaps to the tube. This forms the trumpet.

In the middle of the paper use a marker to write, "Jesus Is Born." The paper should stand tall and not wide, as you write the message. (See the illustration as a guide.)

WHAT YOU DO

1. Give each child a paper with the words "Jesus Is Born." Encourage the children to draw stripes and other decorations on the sign to resemble a flag.

2. Help the children glue the top edge of the flag to the trumpet, using the illustration as a guide.

3. Show the children how to make trumpet sounds in their trumpet.

WHAT YOU TALK ABOUT

Why is Jesus' birth such an important
    announcement to make?
Jesus is the King of kings. People often announce
    the birth of a new king with trumpets.

WANT TO DO MORE?

Play worship music and let the children play their trumpets as you worship. Arrange for the children to form a procession during the church service where they can march to the front of the church, blowing their trumpets. When they stand at the front of the church, they can say in unison, "Jesus is born!" Then they can all march out again, blowing on their trumpets.

Wreath

Shepherds Tell About Jesus' Birth (Luke 2)

WHAT YOU NEED
pictures from p. 146 or pictures cut
    from old story papers or
    nativity cards
11"x 18" green construction paper
bows (1 per child)
yarn
hole punch
crayons
scissors
glue

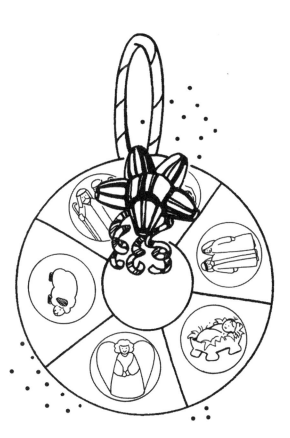

WHAT YOU PREPARE
Duplicate the pictures from page 146 for each child,
or cut out pictures from old story papers or
nativity cards.

Cut a 9" circle from the green paper, one per child.

Cut out a 3 1/2" circle from the center to form
the wreath.

WHAT YOU DO
1. Give each child a copy of the pictures from page
146 to color and cut out. Or provide the pictures cut
from nativity cards and old story papers.

2. Give each child a wreath and a bow. Show the
children how to glue the bow at the top of the
wreath.

3. The children may choose which pictures they want
to use to decorate their wreaths. They don't have to
use all of the pictures. Glue the pictures around the
wreath.

4. Punch a hole at the top of the wreath and tie on a
yarn hanger.

WHAT YOU TALK ABOUT
How do you feel when you think about Jesus' birth?
Who can you tell about Jesus' birth today?

WANT TO DO MORE?
To form a sturdier wreath, purchase green paper
plates. Cut out the center of the paper plates to form
the wreath. Or you can use white plates and paint
them green.

Letter

Shepherds Tell Others (Luke 2)

WHAT YOU NEED
pictures on p. 146
clear tape or glue
crayons
scissors

WHAT YOU PREPARE
Duplicate several copies of the pictures for each child. You will need only the pictures of the shepherds, sheep, angel, and baby Jesus.

Prepare a letter telling about Jesus' birth, leaving room for the children to glue the pictures in the appropriate spaces. Duplicate the letter so that each child can have a copy.

An (picture of angel) appeared to some (picture of shepherds) who were watching their (picture of sheep). The (picture of angel) said, "Do not be afraid. I have good news. A Savior has been born! You will find (picture of baby Jesus) wrapped in cloths and lying in a manger." The (picture of shepherds) hurried to Bethlehem. They found (picture of baby Jesus) just as the (picture of angel) had told them. (Picture of shepherds) told the good news to everyone they saw.

WHAT YOU DO
1. Give each child a letter. Help them cut out and glue the pictures in the appropriate places. If time permits, they may color the letter and pictures.

2. After the children have completed their letters, read the story several times to the children, letting them say the words that the pictures stand for.

WHAT YOU TALK ABOUT
Who did the shepherds tell about Jesus' birth?
Who can you tell about Jesus' birth?

Game of Thanks

Simeon and Anna Thank God (Luke 2)

WHAT YOU NEED
game instructions from p. 146
paper
large-sized paper plates
poster board
paper fasteners
hole punch
crayons
scissors
glue

WHAT YOU TALK ABOUT
What did Simeon and Anna say to God
   when they saw Jesus?
It's important to tell people thank-you
   for gifts.
Let's tell God thank-you for giving us the
   gift of Jesus' birth.

WHAT YOU PREPARE
Draw a circle the size of the paper plates on a piece of white paper. Divide the circle into six pie-shaped sections.

Label each section:
Thank you, God, for Jesus.
Thank you, God, for the Bible.
Thank you, God, for my family.
Thank you, God, for Jesus' birth.
Thank you, God, for church.
Thank you, God, for my friends.

Duplicate the circle so that each child can have a copy. Also make a copy of the game instructions for each child.

Use the poster board to cut a 1" x 4" pointed spinner for each child.

Use the hole punch to punch a hole in the center of each spinner.

WHAT YOU DO
1. Give each child a copy of the circle game and instructions to color and cut out.

2. Show the children how to glue the circle game to the bottom of the plate. They may glue the instructions to the top of the plate.

3. Use the scissors to poke a hole in the center of the game as shown. Mount the spinner to the game with a paper fastener.

4. Let the children play the game in small groups as time permits.

Sewing Card

Wise Men Worship Jesus (Matthew 2)

WHAT YOU NEED

nativity cards with a Christian
   theme (recycled ones are fine)
hole punch
yarn in red, green, or white colors
scissors
clear tape

WHAT YOU PREPARE

Cut the pictures off the front of the cards. Make at least one per child with several extra to choose from.

Punch holes all around the pictures, spaced 1" evenly apart. Be sure that one of the holes is in the top center of the card.

Tie a 4' length of yarn to the top, center hole. Leave a 4" tail of yarn for making the hanger when done.

Wrap tape around the other end of the yarn to make a needle.

WHAT YOU DO

1. Help the children lace around the card, being careful to pull the yarn the entire way through before going through the next hole.

2. When the child has brought the yarn back to the beginning hole, tie a knot in the yarn. Tie the ends of the yarn to form a hanger. Trim the excess.

3. Write the child's name and date on the back of the card.

WHAT YOU TALK ABOUT

Why is Jesus' birth so special?
When we give gifts to others, we remember that
   God gave us the gift of Jesus' birth.

WANT TO DO MORE?

Have the children wrap their ornaments as a gift to give to their parents or grandparents.

Marionette

Wise Men Worship Jesus (Matthew 2)

WHAT YOU NEED
pattern on p. 147
poster board
jumbo craft sticks
paper fasteners
crayons
scissors
clear tape
hole punch
glue

WHAT YOU PREPARE
Duplicate the pattern for each child. Glue the pattern to poster board and cut out the pictures. Punch holes in the two arms and two shoulders as shown.

WHAT YOU DO
1. Give each child the three pieces to make the marionette. Have the children color the marionette.

2. Help the children assemble the marionette by attaching two paper fasteners to the shoulders as shown.

3. Glue the marionette to a craft stick.

WHAT YOU TALK ABOUT
Who did the wise men give their presents to?
Who can you give presents to?
What will you tell that person about Jesus?

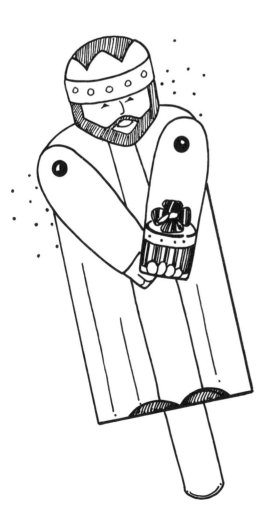

WANT TO DO MORE?
Retell the story, inviting children to stand in front with their marionettes representing the wise men.

Offering Box

Jesus Grows Up (Luke 2)

WHAT YOU NEED

figures and windows on p. 148
tissue box: empty, square, and with a
    top opening (1 per child)
clear, stiff plastic such as from report
    covers or disposable dessert trays
clear tape
scissors
crayons
craft glue

WHAT YOU PREPARE

Duplicate the figures and windows for each child.

Cut away one side of each tissue box, leaving at
least a 1/2" edge the whole way around.

Cut away any plastic that might be in the top
opening of the box.

Cut the clear plastic to fit over the opening in the
tissue boxes, about 4 1/2" x 5" in size, depending on
the size of the boxes.

WHAT YOU DO

1 Give each child the figures and windows to color
   and cut out.

2 Show the children where to glue the pictures of
   Jesus, the Pharisees, and the windows along the
   walls inside the tissue box.

3 Glue the clear plastic over the opening on the side
   of the box. Use a piece of tape along each side to
   hold the plastic in place.

WHAT YOU TALK ABOUT

How did Jesus obey His parents?
How can you obey your parents?

WANT TO DO MORE?

Encourage the children to use the boxes at home to
collect offering to bring to church. You can make a
large box to use in the classroom to collect the
offering each week.

Dove Decoration

John Baptizes Jesus (Matthew 3; John 1)

WHAT YOU NEED

paper
spring-type clothespins
   (1 per child)
feathers
crayons
scissors
glue

WHAT YOU PREPARE

Use the bird in the illustration as a guide to draw a bird shape. Duplicate the bird for each child in your class.

WHAT YOU DO

1. Give each child a bird to color and cut out.

2. Let the children glue a feather or two on their birds.

3. Glue each bird to a clothespin so that the opening of the clothespin is at the top of the bird as shown.

WHAT YOU TALK ABOUT

Who in our story knew that Jesus is God's Son?
What did God send to show that Jesus is His Son?

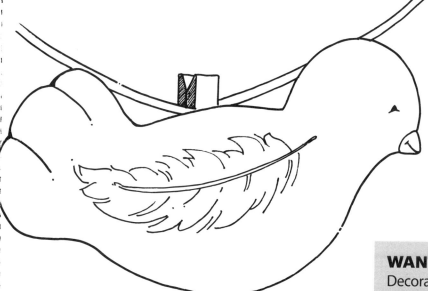

WANT TO DO MORE?

Decorate the classroom with the doves by clipping them to curtains or to a string hanging across the top of the walls. When the doves are ready to go home, ask each child to choose one person to tell that Jesus is God's Son.

Door Stop

Satan Tempts Jesus (Matthew 4)

WHAT YOU NEED
paper
plastic liter soda bottle and lid
   (1 per child)
sand or tiny pebbles such as fish
   tank gravel
funnel
crayons
scissors
glue

WHAT YOU PREPARE
Print "I will follow Jesus" on a sheet of paper and draw simple illustrations, if you wish, of ways children can follow Jesus. Duplicate a paper for each child in the class. Wash the bottles and remove their labels. Fill the bottles partly with sand or gravel. Glue on the lids.

WHAT YOU DO
1. Give each child a picture to color and cut out. Show them how to glue the picture to the bottle.

2. Demonstrate how the bottle works as a doorstop.

WHAT YOU TALK ABOUT
What did Jesus do when Satan tempted Him?
When are you tempted to do wrong?
What will you do to follow Jesus?

Doll of Myself

Jesus' First Followers (John 1)

WHAT YOU NEED

pattern on p. 147
individual-sized plastic water
    bottles (1 per child)
plastic spoons (1 per child)
colorful crew socks (1 per child)
construction paper in a variety
    of colors
ads or magazines with pictures
    of people
buttons, ribbons, or
    other accessories
clear tape
scissors
glue

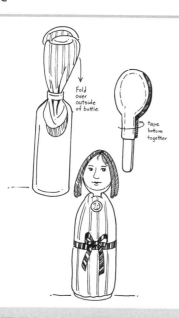

WANT TO DO MORE?

Instead of using magazine pictures to glue on the faces, ask the children to bring in a disposable photograph of themselves from home. Explain that the pictures should be large enough to cut out their faces, such as school pictures. Keep several magazines handy for visitors or children who can't bring a photograph.

WHAT YOU PREPARE

Use the pattern to cut out one shape per child from flesh-toned construction paper.

Cut a variety of faces from the magazines or ads. Be sure to include the ethnic variety of the population in your classroom. Try to make each face at least 2" round.

Turn all the socks inside out.

WHAT YOU DO

1. Give each child a water bottle and a sock. Show the children how to stuff the foot end of the sock inside the bottle. Help them pull the ankle of the sock out over the bottle to form the body of the doll.

2. Fold the construction paper pattern over a plastic spoon and tape the paper around the base of the handle. Let the children choose which face they want to glue to the face of their dolls. The children can cut out hair if they want to add it to their dolls.

3. When the faces are finished, put some glue into the opening of the bottle and stick the handle of the spoon into the bottle, using the illustration of the completed doll as a guide.

4. Decorate the body of the dolls with buttons or bows.

WHAT YOU TALK ABOUT

Why did people in the Bible follow Jesus?
Why do you want to follow Jesus?

Banner of Encouragement

Jesus Teaches About God (John 3)

WHAT YOU NEED

roll paper
paint supplies or washable markers

WANT TO DO MORE?

On a piece of construction paper, trace each child's hand and cut out the handprint. Write "I am praying for (leader's name)" in the center of each handprint. Encourage the children to take the handprints home, hang them on the refrigerator, and pray for the leader each time they see them.

WHAT YOU PREPARE

Cut a sheet of roll paper large enough to have all the handprints of the children in your classroom on the sign. (If you have a very large class, make several banners.)

With large letters, write "We're Praying For You (leader's name)" in the center of the banner.

Prepare a workstation for the children to make handprints and sign their names on the banner.

WHAT YOU DO

1. On the banner, let each child make a handprint with paints or by tracing their hands with marker. Help them sign their names.

2. When the banner is dry, invite the leader to your classroom to present the banner as a gift.

WHAT YOU TALK ABOUT

How was Jesus a friend to Nicodemus?

Water Bottle

Jesus Is a Friend to a Woman from Samaria (John 4)

WHAT YOU NEED
paper
individual-sized plastic bottle
of water with lids (the bottles
may be new, unused, and full of
water; or you can fill the bottles
with fresh water)
crayons
scissors
glue

WHAT YOU PREPARE
Make labels for the bottles by printing John 4:13, 14 on a piece of paper. Enlarge and copy the picture of Jesus from below or use another picture of Jesus. Duplicate the label so that each child can have a copy.

WHAT YOU DO

1. Give each child a label to color. Have children cut the labels to fit their bottles.

2. If the bottles are empty, let the children help you fill them with water.

3. Glue the pictures to the water bottles as labels. Ask the children to choose one friend to give the water bottle to.

WHAT YOU TALK ABOUT
How was Jesus a friend to the Samaritan woman? What can we do to show Jesus' love to our friends?

The Galilee News

Jesus Heals an Official's Son (John 4)

WHAT YOU NEED
paper
headlines cut from newspapers
crayons

WHAT YOU PREPARE
Print "THE GALILEE NEWS" and "EXTRA! EXTRA!" at the top of a piece of paper. Then print "One time Jesus helped me when" as shown in the illustration. Make a copy of the paper for each child in your class.

WHAT YOU DO

1. Give each child a copy of the blank newspaper. Children can draw a picture of how Jesus helped the sick boy, or they can draw a picture of a time Jesus helped them.

2. Let children choose words from the newspaper headlines to glue on for a title to their stories, if they wish.

3. Allow children to share their pictures and stories.

WHAT YOU TALK ABOUT
Let's tell Jesus thank you for helping each one of us.
Could anyone else heal the sick boy?
Why could Jesus heal the sick boy?

WANT TO DO MORE?
Make a classroom newspaper by collecting the children's pictures. To make the newspaper, type descriptions of the ways Jesus helped in the pictures and who drew each picture. Print out this page. Duplicate several of the pictures and reduce them. Cut these pictures out and paste them around the edge of the paper with the sentences on it. Duplicate this and distribute it next week as a classroom newspaper. Return the pictures to the children.

Fishing Rod

Jesus Chooses Four Followers (Mark 1; Luke 5)

WHAT YOU NEED
18"-long slender stick or dowel rod
foam tray such as used for meat
    or vegetables
yarn
large paper clips
magnetic strips
flat buttons
glue
scissors

WHAT YOU PREPARE
Cut a 4"-long fish for each child from the foam trays.
Cut a 2' length of yarn for each child. Cut the magnets into 1/2"x 1" strips.

WHAT YOU DO
1. Give each child a foam fish, a magnetic strip, and a flat button. Show the children how to glue a magnet on the fish for a mouth and a button for the eye. Set aside to dry.

2. Help the children tie one end of the yarn to the stick to form a fishing pole. Tie the paper clip to the other end of the yarn.

3. When the fish has dried, let the children spend time trying to catch their fish.

WHAT YOU TALK ABOUT
How was Jesus a friend to the fishermen?
Who will you tell that Jesus loves them?

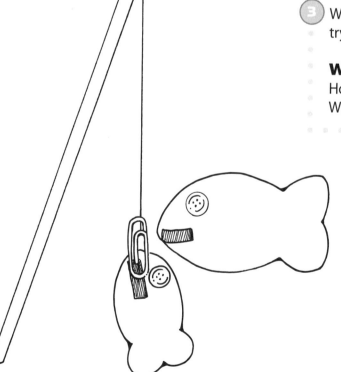

WANT TO DO MORE?
Write small notes of encouragement on small pieces of paper such as "Jesus loves you" and "Jesus is Lord." Glue one note on the back of each fish. Let each child make several fish with different notes on the back of each one. Encourage the children to share their fishing rods with friends and let their friends keep the fish that are caught. Explain that this would be a good way to tell their friends about Jesus.

Flannel Board

Jesus Is a Friend to a Man Who Is Paralyzed (Mark 2)

WHAT YOU NEED

figures of Jesus, the man, and the
 mat from p. 149
felt
cardboard or poster board
crayons
scissors
glue

WHAT YOU PREPARE

Duplicate the figures, 1 set for each child.

Cut the cardboard into 9" x 12" rectangles, one per child. Cut matching rectangles of felt.

Cut 2" x 6" pieces of felt, three per child.

WHAT YOU DO

1. Give each child a copy of the figures to color and cut out. Have the children glue their three pictures to the three small rectangles of felt.

2. Show the children how to glue the large piece of felt to the cardboard to form the flannel board.

3. When the flannel board and pieces are dry, let the children tell the Bible story to each other.

WHAT YOU TALK ABOUT

How can we be a friend to someone who is sick? Let's thank Jesus for showing us how to be a friend.

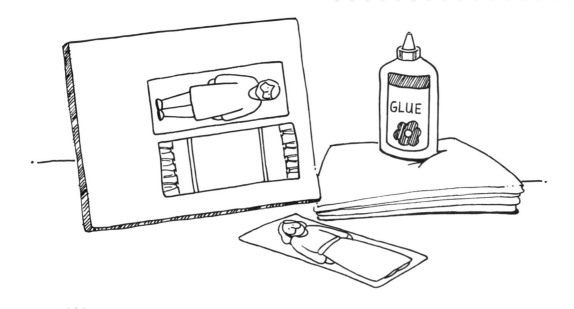

Lift-the-Flap Book

Jesus Heals a Man at a Pool (John 5)

WHAT YOU NEED

3 figures on p. 148, 1 figure on
   p. 149
paper
glue
crayons
scissors

WHAT YOU PREPARE

Photocopy and cut out the figures from pages 148 and 149. Draw the fold and cut lines for the book on two sides of a piece of paper as shown in the illustration. Print the story poem on the pages of the book as shown and glue the figures on the pages. Make photocopies of the book for the children.

Page 1—Sick man, sad man, lying on his mat.
Page 2—Jesus walked by and saw where he sat.
Page 3—"You're healed!" Jesus said. "I'm healed!" said the man.
Page 4—Then he jumped up, danced around … (lift up flap) and off he ran!

WHAT YOU DO

1. Give each child a photocopied book to color.

2. Show the children how to make a cut on the solid line.

3. Help children fold their books correctly, and show them how to fold and lift the flap on page 4.

4. Read through the books in unison several times with the children until they memorize the short poem.

WHAT YOU TALK ABOUT

Jesus wants to help people who are sick.
Jesus makes wonderful things happen because He is very powerful.

side one (front of 8½ x 11)

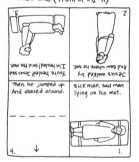

side two (back of 8½ x 11)

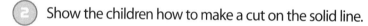
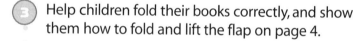
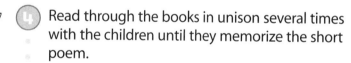

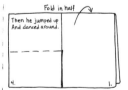
Fold in half

Fold again

Front of book

Wake-up Puppet

Jesus Brings a Young Man Back to Life (Luke 7)

WHAT YOU NEED

lunch-sized paper bags (preferably
    solid colored)
construction paper in a variety
    of colors including red
crayons
scissors
glue

WHAT YOU PREPARE

Cut out 1 1/2" and 1" circles for eyes.

Cut out 2" smiles from red paper.

Cut out 5" x 5" T-shirt shapes from construction
paper that will fit on the bag.

Cut out a variety of 2" x 5" hair shapes.

Cut two black or brown 1 1/2" x 1" rectangles for a
pair of eye lashes. Snip along one edge of each rectangle to form the eye lashes.

WHAT YOU DO

1. Give each child a paper bag. Show them how to lift
   the flap of the bag and glue the eyes underneath
   the flap.

2. Using the illustration as a guide, help the children
   decorate their puppets. Add eyelashes to the bag's
   flap to look like the puppet is asleep. Some children may want to cut out their own hair, T-shirts, or
   mouths from the construction paper.

3. Practice wearing the puppet on your hands and
   making the puppet wake up.

WHAT YOU TALK ABOUT

How did Jesus help the widow and her son?
How did Jesus help you this week?

Soap Gift

Jesus Is a Friend to a Woman Needing Forgiveness (Luke 7)

WHAT YOU NEED
1 bar of soap for each child
fabric
1/4 " fabric ribbon
stickers with a biblical theme
scissors

WHAT YOU PREPARE
Cut the fabric into 10" squares, or squares large enough to wrap around the soap as shown in the illustration.

WHAT YOU DO
1. Give each child a bar of soap. Let them choose a sticker to decorate the top of the soap.

2. Show the children how to place the soap in the center of the fabric square and gather the edges of the fabric together at the top.

3. Tie a ribbon around the fabric.

WHAT YOU TALK ABOUT
When Jesus forgives someone, He washes away their sins.
Is there something you want to tell Jesus you're sorry for?

WANT TO DO MORE?
Encourage the children to give the soap as a gift. They can tell today's story about forgiveness to the person who receives the gift.

Stormy Seas

Jesus Stops a Storm (Mark 4)

WHAT YOU NEED
octopus and anchor patterns from
  p. 150
cereal box (1 per child)
white and blue construction paper
poster board
hole punch
paper fasteners
crayons
scissors
glue

WHAT YOU PREPARE
Duplicate the patterns. Make enough patterns
of the octopus, fish, and anchor for each child to
choose one to use in their project.

Cut the front and sides away from each cereal box,
leaving a 2"-high rim around the bottom as shown.

Cut a 1/2" x 3" slit in the bottom of the cereal box
as shown.

Use the illustration as a guide to cut a triangular sail,
a fish, and a rounded boat bottom from the leftover
cereal box pieces. For each child, cut a 1" x 12" strip
of poster board.

Cut a 3" x 7" white cloud and a 3" x 7" strip of water
for each child.

WHAT YOU DO

1 Give each child a strip of cardboard, the cardboard
sail, and the cardboard boat bottom. Decorate the
sail and the boat. Let the children choose an
octopus, fish, or anchor to color and cut out.

2 Help the children glue the sail, boat, and fish/
anchor/octopus to the strip of cardboard as shown.

3 Glue the cloud and the wave to the cereal box. Use
the scissors or a hole punch to poke a hole in the
boat bottom and in the cereal box as shown.

4 Slip the animal/anchor through the slit in the bottom of the cereal box and mount the boat to the
water with a paper fastener.

WHAT YOU TALK ABOUT
Who is more powerful than a storm?
Jesus wants to use His power to help us.

Kite

Jesus Heals Jairus's Daughter (Mark 5)

WHAT YOU NEED
11" x 18" construction paper
streamers
yarn
washable markers
crayons
scissors
hole punch
clear tape
glue

WHAT YOU PREPARE
Cut the streamers into 1' lengths, two for each child.

WHAT YOU DO

1. Give each child a sheet of construction paper. Show how to fold the paper in half lengthwise and then open it up flat again.

2. Follow the step-by-step instructions to help the children fold the kite. First fold each top corner into the center. Encourage the children to crease the paper well.

   Fold the bottom corner over as shown.

   Fold the other bottom corner over as shown, tucking under the excess edge.

3. Help the children glue the flaps down. Glue two streamers on as a tail.

4. Put a piece of clear tape on the top point of the kite and then use a hole punch to punch a hole over the tape. Tie on a 2' yarn string through the hole.

WHAT YOU TALK ABOUT
Why is Jesus' power so special?
When we feel the power of the wind as we fly our kites, we are reminded of Jesus' power.

Fish Plate

Jesus Feeds 5,000 (John 6)

WHAT YOU NEED
7" colorful paper plate
poster board
construction paper in a variety
  of colors
crayons
scissors
glue

WHAT YOU PREPARE
Use the illustration below to guide you as you trace several fins, tails, and heads onto poster board. Cut these out for the children to use while tracing.

WHAT YOU DO
1. Help the children use the poster board shapes to each trace fins, tail, and head from different colors of construction paper. Have them cut out these shapes.

2. Glue the fin, head, and tail to the back of the paper plate.

3. Draw an eye and a mouth on the fish's head.

WHAT YOU TALK ABOUT
Why could only Jesus feed 5,000 people with five loaves of bread and two fish?
What can we say to thank Jesus for His power?

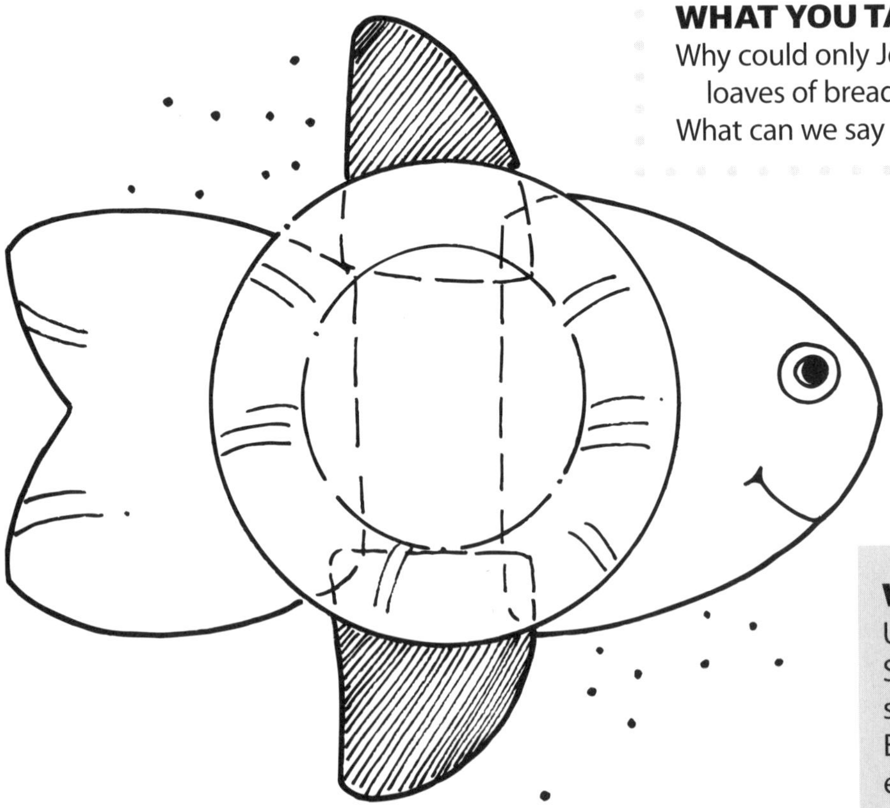

WANT TO DO MORE?
Use the plates during snack time. Serve fish crackers in baskets. Also serve small pieces of bread in baskets. Encourage the children to help serve each other.

Scripture Cards Cup

Jesus Walks on Water (Matthew 14)

WHAT YOU NEED
disposable cups (1 per child)
light-colored construction paper
colored pencils
stickers
crayons
scissors

WHAT YOU PREPARE
Cut the construction paper into small rectangles, approximately 2" x 3". Cut at least five cards for each child.

Print and photocopy the following Scriptures about God's power. Psalm 111:6; Daniel 2:20; Revelation 19:1; 1 Chronicles 29:12; Job 26:14.

WHAT YOU DO

1. Give each child five cards and Scriptures about God's power. Guide children to cut out and glue the Scriptures to the cards.

2. Encourage the children to decorate their cups with stickers.

3. Place the Scripture cards about God's power in the cup. Read each Scripture aloud, explaining what it means.

WHAT YOU TALK ABOUT
What did Jesus do that showed His power in today's story?
We can learn more about Jesus' power when we read the Bible.

Super Hero Cape

Jesus Heals a Man Who Can't Hear (Mark 7)

WHAT YOU NEED
24" x 26" piece of fabric
    (1 piece per child, an old sheet
    works fine)
1/2" or 1"-wide fabric ribbon
felt
craft glue
waxed paper
scissors

WHAT YOU PREPARE
Use the illustration below to guide you to cut out a felt diamond shape and letter from contrasting colors of felt, one of each per child. The shape and letter should be approximately 7" high.

Snip a slit about I" away from the edge in the top two corners of the cape. Tie an 18" piece of ribbon in each slit to use to tie on the cape. Use the illustration as a guide.

WHAT YOU DO
1. Let the children choose two contrasting colors of felt pieces to assemble their super hero logo. Glue the letter to the top of the diamond shape as shown in the illustration.

2. Glue the logo to the back, top center of the cape. Place over waxed paper to protect the surface of the table as it dries. It may need to dry overnight.

WHAT YOU TALK ABOUT
Who has more power than any super hero?
Let's wear our super hero capes and tell others
    about Jesus, the most powerful one in
    the universe.

WANT TO DO MORE?
Keep the capes to dry. Next week, let the children wear their capes and stand in a circle. A volunteer can stand in the middle and say, "I'm a super hero and I want to tell you about Jesus, the most powerful one in the universe!" Encourage the volunteer to say one example of Jesus' power and then pretend to zoom, jump, or flex his muscles to show how much power Jesus has. Have everyone in the circle copy the motion. Repeat the game.

Footprints

Jesus with Moses and Elijah (Matthew 17)

WHAT YOU NEED
pair of men's shoes
12" x 18" construction paper
crayons
scissors
glue

WHAT YOU PREPARE
Trace the men's shoes to make a set of Jesus' footprints for each child.

WHAT YOU DO
1. Give each child a pair of Jesus' footprints to color and cut out.

2. Help the children trace their shoes onto construction paper and cut out their two footprints.

3. Show the children how to glue the four footprints to the construction paper so that their footprints are following Jesus'.

WHAT YOU TALK ABOUT
How did God show that Jesus is His Son in today's story?
How will you follow Jesus because He is the Son of God?

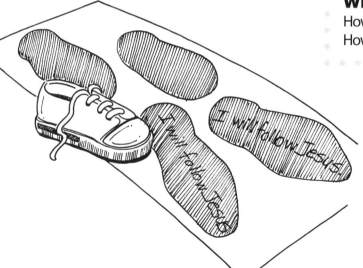

WANT TO DO MORE?
Bring paints and large cake pans. Spread a thin layer of paint in a cake pan. Help each child remove her shoes and socks, step carefully into the paint, and take two steps onto a sheet of paper. The child should then step into a tub of warm, sudsy water and then step out onto a towel for drying. After their feet are dry, the children can glue Jesus' footprints in front of their own footprints on the paper. Use longer sheets of roll paper if you want to let the children make several painted footprints.

Candy Magnet

Jesus Heals a Man Who Can't See (John 9)

WHAT YOU NEED
Scripture strip on p. 150
assortment of candy wrapped
    in individual packages whose
    paper isn't see-through
    (1 per child)
magnetic strips
cotton balls
sandwich-sized plastic bags
curling ribbon
glue
clear tape
scissors
crayons

WHAT YOU PREPARE
Duplicate the Scripture strip for each child.

Carefully cut a slit in the back of each candy wrapper. Remove the candy from the wrapper.

WHAT YOU DO
1. Give each child a pattern to color and cut out.

2. Help the children carefully put a cotton ball inside the empty candy wrapper. Glue the wrapper closed and tape shut.

3. Glue a 1" magnetic strip to the back of the candy wrapper to form the magnet.

4. Have the children wash their hands and help wrap the pieces of candy in individual sandwich-sized bags and tie with a ribbon. Put a Scripture strip in each bag.

WHAT YOU TALK ABOUT
What did Jesus do for a blind man?
What good things has Jesus done for you this week?

WANT TO DO MORE?
Encourage the children to take the candy home and hang the magnet on their refrigerator with the Scripture verse. As they eat the candy or share it with a family member, they can taste the goodness of the candy and remember how good Jesus really is!

Heating Pack

Jesus Teaches About Helping (Luke 10)

WHAT YOU NEED
pretty crew sock with no holes
    (1 per child)
uncooked rice
get well card (purchased or can be
    made from construction paper)
scoop or wide-mouthed funnel
crayons
scissors
glue

WHAT YOU PREPARE
Print the following instructions and duplicate for each child. Instructions for heating: Place in micro-wave for one minute. Do not overheat as rice will burn. Use caution because this will become warm.

WHAT YOU DO

1. Give each child the instructions and a get well card. Have the children color the instructions, cut them out, and glue them inside the cards.

2. Let the children each choose a sock and scoop one cup of uncooked rice into the sock. Tie a knot in the top of the sock so that the rice is loose inside the sock.

3. Tell the children to give their socks to someone they know isn't feeling well. Explain that an adult needs to warm the sock in a microwave so that it will be warm. The warm sock can be used as a heating pack to comfort the person who is sick.

WHAT YOU TALK ABOUT
Who helped the man in Jesus' story?
Who can you help?

Prayers in a Pocket

Jesus Teaches About Prayer (Matthew 6; Luke 11)

WHAT YOU NEED

8 1/2" x 11" construction paper in a variety of colors

short cardboard tube such as from toilet paper (1 per child)

gift wrap

stapler

washable markers

crayons

scissors

glue

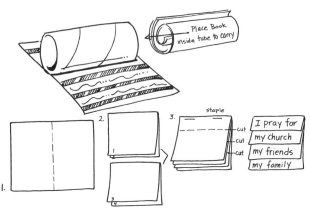

WHAT YOU PREPARE

Cut the gift wrap into 5" x 6" pieces, or a size that fits the cardboard tubes.

Cut the construction paper in half lengthwise. Fold each of these pieces in half and place one inside the other.

Staple along the fold to form a type of book. Cut the first three pages of the book as shown in the illustration.

Label the pages with a marker as shown in the illustration.

WHAT YOU DO

1. Give each child a piece of gift wrap and a cardboard tube. Have the children glue the gift wrap around the cardboard tube. Set aside to dry.

2. Give each child a book. Encourage them to draw a picture of their church, friends, and family on each page.

3. Help the children roll up the prayer book and slip it into the cardboard tube. These prayer books can be tucked in a pocket to carry home.

WHAT YOU TALK ABOUT

What are some things Jesus said when He talked to God?

Let's talk to God now. We can say some of the same things Jesus said.

WANT TO DO MORE?

Sit with the children in your class. Ask them to share their pictures and describe their prayer requests for the people they have included in their prayer books. Take time to pray together for the different requests.

Watering Can

Jesus Teaches About Sharing (Luke 12)

WHAT YOU NEED
2-liter bottles with lids (1 per child)
clear adhesive covering in
bright colors
scissors
nail

WHAT YOU PREPARE
Wash the bottles and lids.

Use the nail to poke about ten holes near the top of one side of the bottle.

Cut the adhesive covering into 3" shapes such as flowers, sunshine, triangles, and circles.

WHAT YOU DO
1 Give each child a plastic bottle and lid to use as a watering can.

2 Let each child choose adhesive-backed plastic shapes to use for decorating their bottles. Help them peel off the backing and stick the shapes around their bottles.

WHAT YOU TALK ABOUT
How can you share with your friends and with your family?
Let's pray and ask Jesus to help us remember to share.

WANT TO DO MORE?
Give each child a packet of seeds to take home. Explain that they are to share these seeds with someone they know. Or, let them plant one sunflower seed in a cup to give to a friend.

Handprint Picture

Jesus Brings Lazarus Back to Life (Luke 10; John 11)

WHAT YOU NEED

11" x 18" construction paper in a
   variety of colors
paints
shallow pans
clean-up supplies
washable markers
scissors
glue

WHAT YOU PREPARE

Each child will need one sheet of construction paper and one paper frame to make his picture. To make the frame, cut the center out of a piece of construction paper, leaving a 1" edge as shown.

Put the paints in shallow pans, one color per pan. Disposable plastic plates with a rim work well.

Prepare a bucket of water and towels to wash paint off hands when finished.

WHAT YOU DO

1   Divide the children into groups of five or less. Give each group at least three shallow pans with paint of different colors.

2   Give each child a sheet of construction paper. Have every child in each group make one handprint on the other children's papers in their group. The children will dip their hand into the paint and then press a handprint on each of the papers in their group. Label each handprint with the child's name.

3   Help the children wash their hands.

4   Glue the frame onto the edge of the picture. Use a marker to write on the frame: "Jesus Gives Us Friends."

WHAT YOU TALK ABOUT

How was Jesus a friend to Lazarus?
How can you be a friend to someone who is feeling sad?

Praise Puppet

Jesus and the Ten Men with Leprosy (Luke 17)

WHAT YOU NEED
puppet patterns on p. 150
empty cereal boxes
   (1 box per 2 children)
construction paper
crayons
scissors
glue

WHAT YOU PREPARE
Duplicate the face and speech balloon patterns for each child.

Cut the cereal box into two 7" x 7" x 10" triangles, using the corners.

Use the pattern to cut two hand and two feet shapes for each child from construction paper.

Cut 1" x 4" strips of paper for the arms and legs.

WHAT YOU DO
1. Give each child a face picture and speech balloon to color and cut out.

2. Help the children trace the box front and the two sides onto construction paper. Cut these pieces out and glue them to cover the front and sides of the box.

3. Use the illustration as a guide to glue on the face, speech balloon, two arms, two hands, two legs, and two feet.

4. Encourage children to wear the Praise Puppets on their hands or sit them on a shelf to help them remember to thank God for His good things.

WHAT YOU TALK ABOUT
How do we feel when someone gives us thanks? How does Jesus feel when we tell Him thank-you? Share something you're thankful for. Let's pray and thank Jesus today.

Necklace

Jesus and the Children (Mark 10)

WHAT YOU NEED
colorful tagboard
12" chenille wire
straws
cereal circles
hole punch
scissors
washable markers

WHAT YOU PREPARE
Use the tagboard to cut one 3" heart and two 2" hearts for each child.

Write "Jesus loves me" on the larger hearts.

Use the hole punch to punch two holes at the top of each heart as shown in the illustration.

Cut the straws into various short lengths.

Twist two lengths of chenille wire together so that they form one long piece. They should overlap about 1".

WHAT YOU DO
1. Give each child a long length of chenille wire, one large heart, and two small hearts.

2. Show the children how to thread the large heart on the necklace to hang in the middle.

3. Let the children string cereal circles, straws, and the two small hearts on the chenille wire.

4. To form a clasp for the necklace, bend back the last 1/2" of each end of the chenille wire. Hook these together to wear the necklace.

WHAT YOU TALK ABOUT
Jesus showed us that He loves children.
We like to spend time with our friends. How can we spend time with our friend, Jesus?

WANT TO DO MORE?
Encourage the children to bring in photographs of themselves. Cut these photographs to fit on the center heart. Glue the photographs in place on the center heart. On the two side hearts write "Jesus Loves Me."

Tree Puppet

Jesus Is a Friend to Zacchaeus (Luke 19)

WHAT YOU NEED
Zacchaeus figure on p. 151
long cardboard tubes such as from
    paper towel rolls (1 per child)
paper plates (1 per child)
green construction paper
stapler
crayons
scissors
glue

WHAT YOU PREPARE
Duplicate the pattern for each child.

Fold the paper plate in half and staple to the top of
the cardboard tube as shown in the illustration. This
forms the tree.

Cut out about ten 3" leaf shapes for each child.

WHAT YOU DO
1. Give each child a picture of Zacchaeus to color and
   cut out.

2. Show the children how to glue Zacchaeus to the
   tree so that he is sitting on the top.

3. Glue green leaves to the tree at random.

WHAT YOU TALK ABOUT
Jesus was a friend to Zacchaeus, even though
    nobody liked Zacchaeus.
After Jesus showed His friendship to Zacchaeus,
    how did Zacchaeus change?
Let's pray and ask Jesus to help us be a friend to
    children who might not be very friendly.

WANT TO DO MORE?
Use the puppets to tell the story of Zacchaeus.
Each time the name Zacchaeus is said, hold the
puppets up high in the air.

Praise Maraca

People Praise Jesus (John 12)

WHAT YOU NEED
lunch-sized paper bags in a
   solid color
small plastic containers with lids
   such as from yogurt, or empty
   aluminum cans
uncooked beans or popcorn
scoop or measuring cup
washable markers
tape
yarn
scissors

WHAT YOU DO
1. Give each child a bag to decorate with markers.

2. Help each child scoop about a cup of dried beans into the plastic container or empty aluminum can. Tape the lid on the container or tape the opening closed on the can.

3. Place the container in the bottom of the bag.

4. Use yarn to tie a handle on the bag to form a maraca.

WHAT YOU TALK ABOUT
What are some things we can do to show worship
   to Jesus?
Why was everyone happy when Jesus rode into
   Jerusalem?

WANT TO DO MORE?
Play lively worship music. Encourage the children to sing along as they shake out a rhythm of praise on their maracas.

Mobile

The Last Supper (Luke 22)

WHAT YOU NEED
fun foam, or poster board, in 3
   different colors (1 color should
   be brown)
paper
chenille wire
hole punch
crayons
scissors
glue

WHAT YOU PREPARE
Draw a 3 1/2" - 4" circle on paper and print Jesus'
words, "Do this in remembrance of me." Duplicate a
circle for each child.

Use the illustration below to guide you to cut a
brown slice of bread and a cup from the foam or
poster board. The figures should be 2 1/2"-3" high.
Cut a foam or poster board circle that is 1" bigger
than the circle pattern.

Use the hole punch to punch holes into the circle,
bread, and cup as shown.

Cut the chenille wire into 6" lengths.

WHAT YOU DO
1. Give each child a paper circle with Jesus' words on it
   to color and cut out.

2. Have the children glue the circle to the circle piece
   of foam or poster board.

3. Help the children use the chenille wire to hang a
   slice of bread and a cup from the bottom of the
   mobile.

4. Help the children use the chenille wire to make a
   hanger at the top of the mobile.

WHAT YOU TALK ABOUT
Jesus asked His friends to remember Him.
The Last Supper helps us remember Jesus and how
   special He is.

Pop-up Flower

Jesus Dies and Lives Again (John 18, 20)

WHAT YOU NEED

9-ounce paper cups (1 per child, not clear)
jumbo craft sticks (1 per child)
construction paper in flower and leaf colors
washable markers
crayons
scissors
glue

WHAT YOU PREPARE

Cut a slit in the bottom of each cup so that a craft stick will slip through.

Cut out 3" flower and leaf shapes.

On the flower shapes, write "Jesus is alive!"

WHAT YOU DO

1. Give each child a craft stick. Show them how to glue a flower and a leaf to the top of the stick. Make sure the leaf is pointing up so that it will fit inside the cup.

2. Slide the bottom of the stick down into the cup and through the slit.

3. Practice popping the flower up out of the cup and saying "Jesus is alive!"

WHAT YOU TALK ABOUT

We feel excited and happy to know that Jesus is alive. What things do we see at springtime to remind us that Jesus is alive? (flowers, animal babies, eggs)

Empty Tomb Rolls

Jesus Is Alive (Matthew 26–28)

WHAT YOU NEED

frozen dinner rolls (1 roll per child)
large marshmallows (1 per child)
oil
sugar
cinnamon
small bowl
aluminum foil
cookie sheets
oven

WHAT YOU PREPARE

Allow the rolls to thaw to room temperature according to the directions on the package.

WHAT YOU DO

1. Help the children wash their hands. If dough is sticky, let the children rub a small amount of oil on their hands.

2. Give each child one roll to pat flat in his hands. Place a marshmallow in the center of each flat circle of dough. Pat the dough up around the marshmallow to form a ball of dough with the marshmallow inside.

3. Roll the ball of dough in a small bowl of cinnamon and sugar until the ball is completely coated.

4. Place the balls of dough on foil-covered cookie sheets. Let the dough rise for 15 minutes. Even if the package says to let the dough rise longer, it's probably unnecessary for this project. Bake the rolls at 350 degrees for 15 minutes until done.

5. Enjoy eating the rolls when they are cool. Surprise! The rolls are empty, just like the tomb was on Easter morning!

WHAT YOU TALK ABOUT

Jesus died, but now He is alive again!
What will you tell a friend about Jesus?

Dinner Rolls

Marshmallow

Marshmallow inside

Church Invitation

The Church Begins (Acts 1, 2)

WHAT YOU NEED
gift wrap
church bulletin
crayons
black permanent marker
scissors
clear tape

WHAT YOU PREPARE
Cut the gift wrap into 12" squares, one per child.

WHAT YOU DO

1. Give each child a square of gift wrap. Use the illustrations and instructions to show the children how to fold the paper into a church.

2. Place the gift wrap face down on the table. Fold the top third over 4" and make a fold.

   Turn the paper over so that the decorated side of the gift wrap is facing you.

   Fold the paper in half as shown and then open out flat again.

   Fold the top two corners down to the center.

   Use scissors to make a 1 1/2" cut on each side as shown.

   Fold in both sides and tape in place.

3. Turn the paper over and draw a church on the front. Write "Join us!" on the front.

4. Encourage the children to give the invitation and a church bulletin to a neighbor or friend.

WHAT YOU TALK ABOUT
Jesus wants us to come to church to learn more about the good news.
Who can we invite to come to church this week?

Fold back

Fold in half / open flat

1½" cut   1½" cut

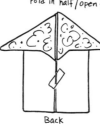
Back

JOIN US!
Front

Offering Can

Peter and John at the Temple (Acts 3)

WHAT YOU NEED
white paper
cardboard can such as from a can
   of peanuts
construction paper
crayons
scissors
glue

WHAT YOU PREPARE
Use the illustration below to draw a simple church shape on paper and duplicate it for each child.

If your class has a lot of younger children or is a large class, cover each can with construction paper before class.

WHAT YOU DO

1. Give each child a church shape to color and cut out.

2. If the cans aren't covered yet, help the children cover the cans by gluing on a strip of construction paper.

3. Glue the picture of the church to the can.

WHAT YOU TALK ABOUT
We help other people when we pray for them.
The church uses our money and our offerings to
   help other people.
When we help others, we are following Jesus' example.

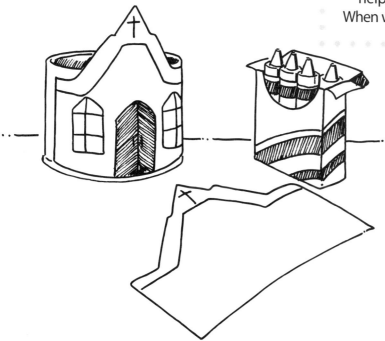

Praying Hands Chain

Peter and John Speak Boldly (Acts 4)

WHAT YOU NEED
hand pattern on p. 151
11" x 18" construction paper in a
    variety of colors
stapler
crayons
scissors

WANT TO DO MORE?
Ask the children to point to their chain of hands hanging around the room. Let them share about the pictures they drew. Spend time praying together for the people they drew in their pictures.

WHAT YOU PREPARE
Fold each piece of construction paper in half lengthwise and cut into two strips.

Fold each strip in half and then two more times to form accordion folds.

Use the pattern as a guide to cut out the shape of a hand from the folded paper.

Make a chain of four hands for each child.

WHAT YOU DO
1. Give each child a chain of hands.

2. Have the children color pictures of the people they choose to pray for.

3. Have the children write their names on their chain of hands. Staple the chains of hands together and hang around the room.

WHAT YOU TALK ABOUT
Who listens to our prayers and answers our prayers? Why is it important for us to pray and ask for God's help?

18"

11"   cut in half

Fold

1.

2.

Good News Book

Philip Teaches a Man from Ethiopia (Acts 8)

WHAT YOU NEED
figures on pp. 151, 152
paper
glitter paint or glitter
sandpaper
cotton balls
blue cellophane or construction
    paper
crayons
scissors
stapler
glue

Glitter Paint

WANT TO DO MORE?
After the books are dry, read them aloud with the children until they memorize the story. Encourage children to read their books to family and friends. Explain that when they share their books, they will be telling other people about Jesus.

WHAT YOU PREPARE
Duplicate the figures for each child.

Divide a piece of paper into fourths to make the four pages of the book. Print the following words on each page.

Page 1—An angel spoke to Philip.
Page 2—Philip met the Ethiopian in the desert.
Page 3—Philip said, "Jesus is the Lamb of God."
Page 4—Good things happen when we tell the Good News!

Glue the correct figure to each page of the book. Then photocopy the book for each child.

Cut the sandpaper and the cellophane into 1" x 3" pieces, one of each for every child.

WHAT YOU DO
1. Give each child a book to cut apart.

2. Help the children add glitter to the picture of the angel, glue the sandpaper to the road, glue the cotton ball to the sheep, and glue the cellophane to the water.

3. Staple the books together along the left side.

WHAT YOU TALK ABOUT
What happened when Philip told the Ethiopian about Jesus?
What might happen when we tell our friends about Jesus?

Sew a Treat

Peter and Tabitha (Acts 9)

WHAT YOU NEED
colorful poster board or tagboard
clear, stiff plastic sheet such as is
    used on report covers or on
    pastry boxes
small hard candies at least 1" in
    diameter
hole punch
yarn
clear tape
scissors

WHAT YOU PREPARE
Cut matching hearts from poster board and the clear plastic. Make one set per child. The hearts should be 5 1/2"-6" across.

Punch holes the entire way around both hearts to form a sewing card.

Tie on a 2' length of yarn at the top of the heart.

Wrap a small piece of tape around the other end of the yarn to form a needle.

WHAT YOU DO
1. Give each child a set of hearts with yarn. Show the children how to sew around the hearts, lacing them together.

2. When the heart is almost sewn closed, insert several pieces of candy inside the pocket that is forming.

3. Sew the heart completely closed, tying a knot at the end.

WHAT YOU TALK ABOUT
How did Tabitha help others?
What can we do to help other people?
Let's pray for someone we know who needs
    God's help.

WANT TO DO MORE?
Encourage the children to give their treats to someone they want to tell about Jesus. Let them practice retelling the Bible story to each other so that they can also tell the story to their other friends.

Learning Lace-up

Paul Learns About Jesus (Acts 9, 22)

WHAT YOU NEED
church pattern from p. 153
lightweight cardboard such as
    file folders
ball of string or yarn
glue
hole punch
scissors
clear tape
crayons

WHAT YOU PREPARE
Copy the church pattern found on page 153, one per child.

Cut a piece of yarn for each child that is long enough to be laced correctly through all of the holes. You may want to dip the ends of the yarn in glue and allow them to dry, or wrap them in tape to prevent fraying.

WHAT YOU DO

1. Give each child a church pattern to color.

2. Help children glue the pattern to lightweight cardboard or a file folder for sturdy backing and have them cut around the picture when the glue is dry.

3. Practice reading through the sentences aloud with the children, guiding them as they locate the corresponding pictures.

4. Use a hole punch to punch out the holes where indicated by the open circles on the pattern.

5. Distribute a piece of yarn to each child and demonstrate how to lace the yarn through the holes in a crossing pattern as they connect the sentences to the corresponding pictures.

WHAT YOU TALK ABOUT
How did Paul learn about Jesus?
Name one way you learn about Jesus.

Good News Bucket

Paul and Barnabas Tell About Jesus (Acts 11, 13)

WHAT YOU NEED

shirt pattern on p. 154
Scripture Card pattern on p. 154 (at least 3 per child)
paper plates (1 per child)
crayons or washable markers
scissors
empty, clean plastic gallon milk or juice jug (1 per child)
stapler
11 x 17-inch construction paper (any color)
black construction paper (1 piece for every 2 children)
white crayon

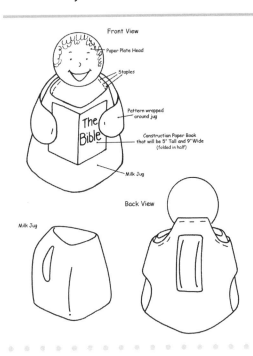

Front View
Paper Plate Head
Staples
Pattern wrapped around jug
The Bible
Construction Paper Book that will be 5" Tall and 9" Wide (folded in half)
Milk Jug

Back View
Milk Jug

WHAT YOU TALK ABOUT

Paul and Barnabas told others about Jesus. Who do you want to share the Good News with today?

WHAT YOU PREPARE

Cut the milk jugs as shown in the illustration below.

Cut sheets of black construction paper in half widthwise so that each piece is 6" tall and 9" wide.

Fold enough sheets of 11 x 17-inch paper in half for every child to have one. Trace the shirt pattern found on page 154 onto each folded piece of paper as indicated on the pattern instructions.

Make enough copies of the Scripture Card found on page 154 for each child to have at least 3.

WHAT YOU DO

1. Give each child a paper plate and crayons or markers. Allow children to decorate the paper plate to look like a face.

2. Give each child a pre-cut plastic milk or juice jug. Allow the children to staple the paper plate faces to the top back portion of the jug as shown in the example.

3. Give each child a shirt pattern and scissors and allow children to cut out the shirt pattern and attach it to the jug using a stapler. Do not attach the arms at this point, only the shoulders and the sides of the shirt.

4. Give each child a pre-cut piece of black construction paper and a white crayon. Children should fold the construction paper in half width-wise to form a book, and write "The Bible" on the cover of the book. Help children attach the books to the arms using a stapler (see the example).

5. Give children several Scripture Cards to place inside their open jugs. Children can use their Good News Buckets to tell others the Good News about Jesus that's found in the Bible.

Pull Through

Paul and Barnabas Help People Know About Jesus (Acts 14)

WHAT YOU NEED

pull-through and word strip
    patterns on p. 155
lightweight cardboard
    (file folders, *optional*)
glue (*optional*)
scissors
crayons

WHAT YOU PREPARE

Copy the patterns for each child. (For extra durability, glue each to lightweight cardboard. Do not glue the strip to cardboard.)

WHAT YOU DO

1. Give each child a pattern of the Pull-Through and Word Strip to color and cut out.

2. Help children cut the two slits as shown in the example.

3. Demonstrate how to weave the word strip through the slits so that the words appear on the front. To do this, children should hold the word strip behind the picture. Weave the top of the word strip through the bottom slit from behind and then through the top slit from the front so that one word at a time appears on the picture when the strip is pulled through.

4. Instruct children to pull the word strip *gently* to reveal each word.

5. Practice reading the sentences aloud.

WHAT YOU TALK ABOUT

Who is Jesus?
What is He like?
Why is it important for people to know that Jesus is God's Son?

Leaves on a Tree

Lydia Follows Jesus (Acts 16)

WHAT YOU NEED
leaf patterns on p. 152
green construction paper
white roll paper
brown roll paper
blue roll paper
construction paper (various colors)
stapler or clear packaging tape
scissors
clear tape
crayons or pencils

WANT TO DO MORE?
Cut out more leaf shapes from green construction paper. Ask children to name other ways they can follow Jesus. Help them write their ideas on the leaves and add them to the tree.

WHAT YOU PREPARE
Copy a set of leaves from page 152 for each child.

Create an outdoor scene on a wall or bulletin board as shown in the example using white roll paper as a background. (If you do not have enough space available, create a smaller scene on piece of poster board.)

To build a 3-D tree trunk with branches, twist long strips of brown roll paper and mount them to the mural or poster board. The branches can be stapled flat against the paper or they can hang freely away from the paper.

WHAT YOU DO
1. Give each child scissors and a set of leaves to cut out.

2. Read the sentences on the leaves aloud and discuss what each sentence means.

3. Tell the children that we can follow Jesus just like Lydia did. Ask the children to choose leaves that they would like to hang on the tree based on the sentences on the leaves and whether they agree with those sentences. Once children have chosen their leaves allow them to hang the leaves on the tree after writing their names on the leaves. The leaves can be attached with tape or a stapler.

WHAT YOU TALK ABOUT
Who told Lydia about Jesus?
What did Lydia do when she chose to follow Jesus?
How will our actions be different when we decide to follow Jesus?

Bible

Paul and Silas Sing in Prison (Acts 16)

WHAT YOU NEED
figure of Jesus from p. 149
11" x 18" black construction paper
   (1 per child)
light colored construction paper
crayons
scissors
glue

WHAT YOU PREPARE
Duplicate the figure of Jesus for each child. If possible, enlarge the pattern.

Print John 3:16 on a slip of paper for each child.

Cut a 1" x 6" strip and a 1" x 8" strip of light paper for each child. These strips will be used to form a cross.

WHAT YOU DO
1. Give each child a picture of Jesus to color and cut out.

2. Give the children each a sheet of black construction paper. Help them fold it in half to resemble a book. This forms the Bible.

3. On the front of the Bible, glue the two strips of paper to form a large cross.

4. On the inside of the Bible, glue the picture of Jesus and a slip of paper with John 3:16 printed on it.

WHAT YOU TALK ABOUT
Sometimes it is hard to tell other people about Jesus.
We can share our Bible with other people when we tell them about Jesus.
Have you ever told someone about Jesus?

Megaphone

Paul Tells a Crowd About Jesus (Acts 21, 22)

WHAT YOU NEED
poster board or tagboard in
   bright colors
washable markers
stapler
scissors
clear tape

WHAT YOU PREPARE
Use the illustration below as a guide to cut out a piece of poster board for each child.

WHAT YOU DO

1. Give the poster board to each child to decorate with markers.

2. After the poster board is decorated, roll the edges together to form a megaphone.

3. Staple and tape the edges in place.

WHAT YOU TALK ABOUT
Sometimes we can tell a lot of people about Jesus at one time.
Have you ever been in a big crowd who is listening to someone speak about Jesus?
Sometimes it might be dangerous for someone to talk about Jesus. There are places in the world today that it might be dangerous to talk about Jesus.

WANT TO DO MORE?
Use megaphones during worship. Let the children sing by using their megaphones. Ask them what it might feel like to try to tell a large group of people about Jesus.

Stand for Jesus

Paul Is Shipwrecked (Acts 27, 28)

WHAT YOU NEED

instant camera or pictures of chil-
    dren from magazines or papers
construction paper
3-ounce paper cups
plaster of paris
craft sticks
plastic spoons
water
crayons
scissors
glue

WHAT YOU PREPARE

If you don't have an instant camera and film, cut full-length pictures of children from magazines or papers. The figures should be approximately 5"- 6" tall.

WHAT YOU DO

1. Take photos of each child or allow each child to choose a picture you have cut out. Guide children to glue their photo or picture of construction paper, print "Jesus is Lord!" by it, and cut around it.

2. Glue each picture onto a craft stick.

3. Follow the instructions on the plaster of paris to mix plaster in the small cups. Make one cup of plaster for each child.

4. As the plaster begins to become firm (this happens in about three minutes), place the craft stick in the center of the cup. Allow this to dry.

WHAT YOU TALK ABOUT

Paul told everyone about Jesus.
We can tell everyone about Jesus too.
Who can you tell about Jesus this week?

Chalkboard Message

Paul Tells About Jesus in Rome (Acts 28; Philippians 1)

WHAT YOU NEED
white paper
black construction paper
jumbo craft sticks (2 per child)
craft sticks (2 per child)
spring-type clothespins
   (2 per child)
scissors
crayons
glue

WHAT YOU PREPARE
Print "Jesus loves you" on a 3" x 5" or smaller rectangle of white paper. Make one for each child.

Cut the black construction paper into 5" x 7" rectangles.

WHAT YOU DO

1. Give each child a piece of black paper, two jumbo craft sticks, and two craft sticks. Show the children how to glue the craft sticks to the edge of the paper, using the illustration as a guide.

2. Give each child a "Jesus loves you" paper to color and glue in the center of the chalkboard.

3. After the craft sticks have dried, clip on two clothespins to use as legs for the chalkboard. (Note: This chalkboard probably won't stand up on its own, but it can be propped up.)

WHAT YOU TALK ABOUT
Why is it important that we tell others about Jesus even if it might be a hard thing to do?
Let's tell our friends and family that Jesus loves them.

Chick and Eggs

Resurrection Sunday

WHAT YOU NEED
wing, beak, and leg patterns from p. 127
strawberry basket (1 per child)
12" yellow paper plate (1 per child)
yellow construction paper
orange construction paper
poster board
large plastic googly eyes
plastic grass
plastic eggs
candy
paper
pen
stapler
glue

WHAT YOU PREPARE
Use the illustration as a guide to staple the plate to the strawberry basket.

Use the pattern to make several wings, beaks, and feet from poster board for the children to use while tracing. (If you have a large class or a lot of younger children, cut the actual wings, beaks, and feet out before class.)

Write "Jesus is alive" on a slip of paper, one per child.

WHAT YOU DO
1. Help the children trace and cut out two wings from yellow paper. Help the children trace and cut out one beak and two feet from orange paper.

2. Staple the wings and feet to the strawberry basket as illustrated.

3. Show the children how to glue the eyes and beak to the center of the plate. Allow the plate to lie flat while the eyes and beak dry.

4. Invite the children to each help you fill several eggs with candy. Put the slip of paper with "Jesus is alive" inside one egg. Place several eggs and plastic grass in each basket.

WHAT YOU TALK ABOUT
How can you celebrate Jesus' resurrection?
Jesus is alive today and loves you very much.

Jesus is Alive!

WANT TO DO MORE?
Fill one plastic egg for each child with uncooked rice. Tape the eggs securely closed with wide clear tape. Let the children use their eggs as rhythm shakers as you worship together with lively music.

Flower Basket

Ressurection Sunday

WHAT YOU NEED
pattern on p. 127
10" paper plates (2 for each child)
poster board, white or green
construction paper in a variety of
   colors for flowers
variety of flat buttons
crayons
scissors
glue

WHAT YOU PREPARE
Duplicate one pattern for each child.

Use the illustration as a guide to cut out half of the center of each plate.

Staple two plates together facing each other to form the basket.

Make several poster board flowers for the children to use for tracing. Use the illustration below as a guide for cutting out flower shapes.

If you have a large class or many younger children, cut most of the flowers out ahead of time. Each child will use about eight flowers.

Cut the poster board into 5", 6", and 7" strips for the stems of the flowers.

WHAT YOU DO
1. Help the children trace the flowers and cut them out. Glue each flower to a poster board stem. Children may glue buttons to the center of the flowers if they choose.

2. Give each child a basket and a pattern to color and cut out. Glue the picture to the basket as shown.

3. When the flowers are dry, stand them up in the basket.

WHAT YOU TALK ABOUT
How do spring flowers remind us that Jesus is alive again? Let's give a flower to a friend and tell her Jesus is alive.

Coupon Bag

Mother's Day

WHAT YOU NEED

coupons on p. 128
lunch-sized paper bag
pretty cotton fabric
construction paper in coordinating
    colors with the fabric
1"-wide ribbon in coordinating
    colors with the fabric
yarn or thin ribbon
hole punch
waxed paper
clear tape
scissors
glue

WHAT YOU PREPARE

Duplicate one set of coupons for each child.

Use the illustration to guide you to cut out two shoes for each child.

Cut the fabric into 7" x 9" rectangles.

WHAT YOU DO

1 Follow the illustration as a guide to show the children how to glue the two shoes at the bottom of the lunch bag. (Fold the flap of the lunch bag to the back of the bag. Glue the shoes at the front of the bag.)

2 Help the children glue the fabric to the top edge of the front of the bag. The fabric will have a pleat in it. Allow the fabric to hang freely. This forms a skirt. (Put waxed paper inside the bag if necessary to keep it from getting glued shut.)

3 Glue a strip of 1"-wide ribbon across the top of the fabric to form the belt of the skirt.

4 To reinforce the back of the bag, put clear tape across the top edge. Punch two holes at the opposite top corners on the back of the bag. Tie on a 15" yarn or ribbon handle.

5 Cut the coupons into strips and place the coupons in the bag. The bag can be hung on a doorknob.

WHAT YOU TALK ABOUT

Helping your mother is one way you show your love
    for her.
Let's say a prayer of thanks to God for giving moth-
    ers and grandmothers.

Mother's Day Card

Mother's Day

WHAT YOU NEED
patterns on p. 156
8 1/2" x 11" construction paper
teabags (1 per child)
crayons
scissors
glue sticks

WHAT YOU PREPARE
Cut the construction paper in half.

Duplicate the patterns for each child. Cut the teacups where indicated on the dotted line.

WHAT YOU DO

1. Give the two pictures to each child to color and cut out.

2. Help the children fold the construction paper in half to form a card. Have them glue the picture on the front of the card.

3. On the inside of the card, glue the picture of the teacup to form a pocket. Be careful to glue only along the two sides and along the bottom of the teacup. Slip the tea bag into the teacup.

4. Help the children sign the card.

WHAT YOU TALK ABOUT
Let's thank God for the people in our families.

Love,
Justin

Mail Basket

Father's Day

WHAT YOU NEED

bear head and paw patterns
   on p. 157
brown construction paper
envelope about 4" x 7" (1 per child)
empty cereal box (1 per child)
crayons
scissors
glue

WHAT YOU PREPARE

Duplicate the bear's face on construction paper for each child.

Cut part of the front, top, and sides off of the cereal box, leaving the entire back and a 3"-high container in front.

Use the pattern to cut out two bear's paws from brown paper for each child.

Glue a piece of brown paper to cover the inside back of the cereal box.

WHAT YOU DO

1. Give a cereal box and an envelope to each child. Help each child write "To: Dad/Grandpa, From: (child's name)" on the front of the envelope.

2. Help the children glue the envelope to the front center of the cereal box.

3. Help the children glue the paws onto the side and front of the cereal box as shown in the illustration. Show them how to glue the face of the bear to the cereal box.

WHAT YOU TALK ABOUT

Let's say a prayer thanking God for dads and grandpas. Who is our heavenly Father?

Father's Day Card

Father's Day

WHAT YOU NEED
patterns on pp. 127, 156
8 1/2" x 11" construction paper
new pencils or pens (1 per child)
crayons
scissors
glue sticks
clear tape

WHAT YOU PREPARE
Duplicate the patterns for each child. Cut along the dotted line on the pencil cup where indicated.

WHAT YOU DO
1. Give each child the pictures to color and cut out.

2. Help the children fold the paper in half to look like a card. On the front of the card, glue the picture of "Happy Father's Day!"

3. Show the children how to glue the pencil cup inside the card to form a pocket. Be careful to only glue the two sides and bottom edge of the picture.

4. After the glue has dried, insert a pencil or pen into the pocket. Hold in place with one piece of tape, if needed.

WHAT YOU TALK ABOUT
What are some ways to show our fathers that we love them?

What are some of the things we like to do with our dads and grandpas?

Hat Pencil Cup

Independence Day

WHAT YOU NEED

cardboard container from nuts or other snacks (1 per child)
different-sized paper plates for tracing circles
construction paper in red, white, and blue colors
star stickers
crayons
scissors
glue

WHAT YOU PREPARE

Cut the red paper into 1"-wide strips.

WHAT YOU DO

1. Help the children cut a piece of white paper to wrap around their containers. Have them spread glue on one side of the white paper. Show them how to glue the white paper around the cardboard containers.

2. Glue the red stripes of paper evenly around the container as shown in the illustration.

3. Have the children use a corresponding plate to trace a circle onto blue paper that is a couple of inches larger than their containers.

4. Cut out the circle, and glue the container on the center of the circle. This forms Uncle Sam's Hat. Decorate the blue paper with star stickers. Put pencils or pens in the hat.

WHAT YOU TALK ABOUT

Let's thank God for America.
Let's say a prayer for the leaders in our country.

Turkey Napkin Holder

Thanksgiving

WHAT YOU NEED
turkey head and feather patterns
   from p. 157
empty cereal box (1 for every 2
   children)
wide, clear tape
construction paper in a variety of
   colors
poster board
napkins
crayons
scissors
glue

WHAT YOU PREPARE
Duplicate the pattern for each child.

Make several feathers from poster board for the
children to use for tracing.

Cut a few feathers out for the children who can't cut
as well. Each child will need about five feathers.

Tape the top and bottom of the cereal box closed.
Cut each box in half around the middle. Trim each
piece to be 4" tall.

If your class is large or you have a lot of younger
children, cover the cereal boxes before class to save
time. Cut a piece of brown construction paper to fit
on each side of the boxes and glue in place.

WHAT YOU DO
1. Give each child a box. If you haven't covered the
   boxes, cut the brown construction paper to fit on
   each side of the boxes. Help the children glue these
   in place.

2. Give each child a picture of the turkey head to color
   and cut out. Let each child choose five feathers or
   trace and cut out five feathers of his own. Help the
   children glue the head and feathers to the box as
   shown.

3. Place several napkins in the box.

WHAT YOU TALK ABOUT
What are you thankful for?
How do we say thank-you to God?

WANT TO DO MORE?
Talk with each child and write down five
things on an index card he is thankful
for. Place the card in the napkin holder.
Encourage the children to say a prayer
of thanks at home during mealtime for
the items on their lists.

Advent tree

Jesus' Birth

WHAT YOU NEED

star pattern from below
7" paper plate, (red or green,
    1 per child)
9-ounce green plastic cup (1 per child)
12" chenille wire (1 per child)
pony beads, 24 per child (or circle-
    shaped candies with the ceners
    cut out)
yellow craft foam or poster board
scissors
hole punch
glue

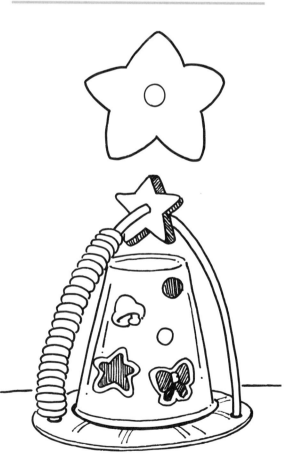

WHAT YOU PREPARE

Punch two holes opposite each other on the rim of each plate.

Use the pattern to cut one star for each child from craft foam or poster board. Punch a hole in the center.

WHAT YOU DO

1. Give each child a paper plate, cup, chenille wire, star, and 24 beads.

2. Help the children glue their cups upside down to the center of their plates. Check that the cups are in the center. The green cup Is supposed to resemble a pine tree.

3. Have the children put 24 beads on their chenille wire. Add the star at the end.

4. Using the illustration as a guide, help the children twist each end of the chenille wire into the opposite holes on the rim of the plate. (If the chenille wire isn't long enough, carefully twist another wire to the first to make it longer.)

5. The chenille wire should form an arch over the top of the cup. Slide the star down to the plate and slide all the beads to be on top of the star.

6. Use the advent tree to count the days until December 25th. Each day, slide one bead over to the opposite side. On the last day, slide the star up. It should be at the top of the green cup and will represent the star on the top of the tree.

WHAT YOU TALK ABOUT

When do you celebrate Jesus' birth?
Why do you look forward to celebrating Jesus' birth?

Tree Growth Chart

Jesus' Birth

WHAT YOU NEED
roll paper (yellow and green)
red and white construction paper
brown construction paper
yarn
clear tape
scissors
glue

WHAT YOU PREPARE
Cut the yellow paper into 1' x 3' pieces, one per child.

Cut six green triangles for each child that measure 10" on each side.

Use construction paper to cut 3" circle ornaments. Each child will need about eight ornaments.

Cut 3" x 12" strips of brown construction paper.

WHAT YOU DO

1. Give each child a strip of yellow paper, a brown strip of paper, and six green triangles. Follow the illustration as a guide to help the children glue the brown strip to the bottom of the yellow paper. This forms the trunk of the tree.

2. Starting at the trunk, glue one green triangle over the top edge of the trunk to make the bottom of the tree. Glue the second green triangle over the first and cover about 2" of the top of the first triangle. Glue the remaining triangles to the yellow paper in the same manner until the top of the tree is glued on.

3. Glue the ornaments on the tree. Try to space them evenly from top to bottom.

4. Tape the back top edge of the yellow paper. Punch two holes at opposite corners of the top edge, through the tape, and tie on a 2' yarn hanger.

5. Hold the tree up against the wall and measure the child's height. Write the child's name, height, and date on the ornament that corresponds with her height.

WHAT YOU TALK ABOUT
As we grow, how can we learn more about Jesus? Let's sing "Happy Birthday" to Jesus.

Fall Wreath

Fall

WHAT YOU NEED
10" paper plate (1 per child)
construction paper in fall colors:
   red, orange, brown, green,
   yellow
hole punch
yarn
scissors
glue

WHAT YOU PREPARE
Cut the center out of each paper plate, making the shape of a wreath.

Cut leaf shapes out of a variety of colors of construction paper, using the illustration below as a guide. Each child will use about 25 paper leaves to make a wreath.

Cut out most of the leaves. Some of the children may want to cut out their own, so let some remain uncut.

WHAT YOU DO
1. Give each child a paper plate wreath. Make sure the bottom of the plate is facing up. It's easier to glue the leaves on this side.

2. Put the pile of leaves in the center of the table for the children to choose from. Show them how to glue their leaves around the wreath.

3. After the wreaths are made, punch a hole in each wreath and tie on a yarn hanger.

WHAT YOU TALK ABOUT
Who makes the leaves turn such a beautiful color? What other beautiful things does God make in our world?

WANT TO DO MORE?
Take a short walk to collect fall leaves in bags. Make a display of the leaves on a table in the classroom. Add a small sign to the display that says, "Thank you, God, for giving us beautiful things."

Snowman Snow Gauge

Winter

WHAT YOU NEED

plastic gallon milk or orange juice jugs
black craft foam or construction paper
white crayons
black flat 1/2" buttons (2 per child)
1/4"-wide red fabric ribbon
rulers, yardsticks, or sticks
   (1 per child)
craft glue
stapler

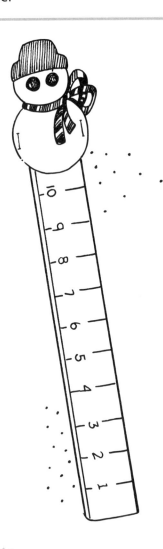

WHAT YOU PREPARE

Use the illustration to cut snowmen from plastic jugs. Each snowman should be approximately 5" high. Cut two snowmen for each child.

Cut a foam hat for each child. Use the illustration as a guide. If you will be using construction paper, make several hats from poster board for tracing.

Cut the ribbon into 12" lengths, one for each child.

Spread craft glue on each snowman shape. Sandwich the last inch of the ruler between the two snowmen. (Make sure the 12" end of the ruler is between the snowmen.) Staple the snowman on each side of the ruler and once at the top of his head. (If using a stick or a yardstick, follow the same directions.)

WHAT YOU DO

1. Give each child a prepared snowman on a ruler. If using construction paper hats, help the children trace the hats with white crayon onto the paper and cut them out.

2. Glue a hat on the head of the snowman. Glue two black buttons on for eyes.

3. Help the children tie a red ribbon around each snowman's neck.

4. Let the snowman lie flat until the buttons are dry.

5. Encourage children to use their gauges to measure the snowfall outside.

WHAT YOU TALK ABOUT

Who created the seasons?
Who designs each snowflake and makes each one unique?
Who creates each person and makes us all special?

Bird Feeder

Spring

WHAT YOU NEED
2 paper bowls (three for every 2 children, use plastic bowls if you want these feeders to last longer)
yarn
stickers of birds
bird seed
scoop for the seed
sandwich-sized plastic bags
twist ties to close bags
hole punch
stapler
scissors
crayons

WHAT YOU PREPARE
Cut one bowl in half.

Using the illustration as a guide, staple the two bowls together along their rims.

Punch two holes on the top rim of the uncut bowl. Tie on a 2' yarn hanger.

WHAT YOU DO

1. Give each child a prepared bird feeder.

2. If using paper bowls, the children may color the bottom of the bowls. Encourage the children to decorate their feeders with the stickers of the birds.

3. Invite the children to help scoop the bird seed into the plastic bags. Tie each bag securely.

4. Put one bag of seed into each feeder.

WHAT YOU TALK ABOUT
Who takes care of the birds?
Who promises to take care of you and me?

Bug House

Summer

WHAT YOU NEED

1/2 -gallon cardboard juice box
   (1 per child)
knee-high stockings (1 per child,
   or cut the legs off a pair
   of stockings)
coffee filter (1 per child)
spring-type clothespins
   (1 per child)
chenille wire
fine-tipped permanent marker
watercolor paints
paint brush
twist ties
scissors
glue

WHAT YOU PREPARE

Cut away one side of the box as shown in
the illustration.

WHAT YOU DO

1. On a protected surface, have each child paint one
   coffee filter in pretty colors.

2. After the coffee filters have dried, form the
   butterflies. Spread glue on the inside closing part
   of each clothespin. Gather the coffee filter in the
   center and clamp this part inside the clothespin.
   Spread the wings.

3. Fold a 6" chenille wire in half. Clamp the center of
   the chenille wire inside the clothespin to form the
   antennae of the butterfly. Apply a little glue to hold
   in place.

4. Use the marker to draw two dots for eyes on
   the butterflies.

5. Have the children place their butterflies inside the
   cardboard boxes. Pull a stocking up over each box.
   Use a twist tie to close the top of the stocking.

WHAT YOU TALK ABOUT

Bugs are very important to our world.
What important jobs did God give bugs when he
   created them?
Which bugs are safe for us to play with?

WANT TO DO MORE?

Take a short walk while the filters are drying.
Find several bugs and put them in a jar. Take these
bugs back to the classroom and observe them.
Set them free at the end of class.

cut at dotted line

Pens

Pencils

Pencils

Pens

Pens

Father's Day Card , page 118

Flower Basket, page 114

Jesus is Alive!

Chick and Eggs, page 113

HAPPY MOTHER'S DAY: I will help with the dishes.

HAPPY MOTHER'S DAY: I will take out the trash.

HAPPY MOTHER'S DAY: I will set the table.

HAPPY MOTHER'S DAY: I will feed the cat/dog.

HAPPY MOTHER'S DAY: I will make my bed.

HAPPY MOTHER'S DAY: I will help you however you want.

HAPPY MOTHER'S DAY: Breakfast in bed.

Coupon Bag, page 115

Underwater Scene, page 9

Animal Hook-Up Game, page 10

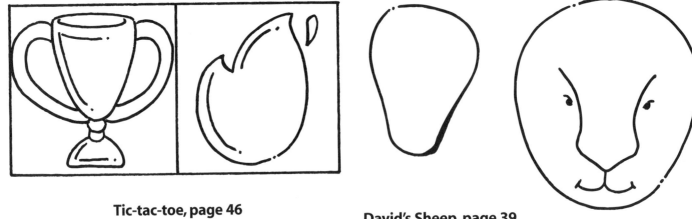

Tic-tac-toe, page 46

David's Sheep, page 39

Baby Moses Basket, page 22

Noah's Ark and Puppets, page 12

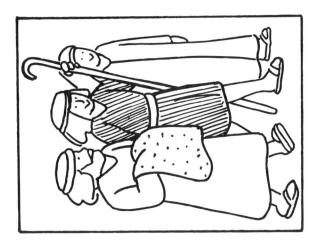
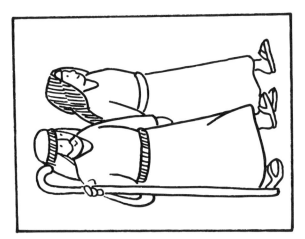

Abraham's Map, page 14

Soccer Game, page 15

Pop-up Puppet, page 40

Jacob's Game, page 19

Forgiveness Lollipop, page 21

I'm sorry.

I forgive you.

Goliath stood so big and tall.
He seemed the strongest of them all.
David wasn't tall, you see,
But he was filled with bravery.
God helped David use his sling
And win the battle for the King.
Down, down, down, down.
Goliath fell down to the ground.
"Hooray!" they cheered. "We won the fight!
God helped David do what's right."

Poem for Pop-up Puppet, page 40

Spyglasses, page 27

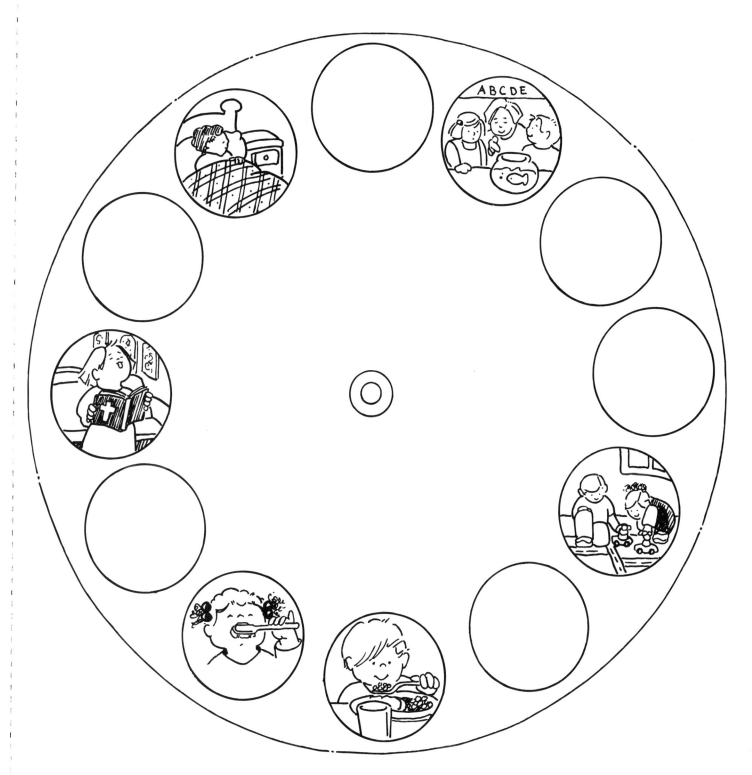

God Cares Clock, page 23

Obey the Lord your God
and follow His commands.

Deuteronomy 27:10

He became the source
of eternal salvation
for all who obey Him.

Hebrews 5:9

We will serve the
Lord our God
and Obey Him.

Joshua 24:24

We know that the
law is good.

1 Timothy 1:8

The Word of the Lord
is right and true.

Psalm 33:4

A new command I give you;
Love one another.

John 13:34

I love your law.

Psalm 119:97

Children, obey your parents
in the Lord,
for this is right.

Ephesians 6:1

Obey me, and I will be
your God and you will be
my people. Walk in all the ways
I command you
that it may go well with you.

Jeremiah 7:23

And this is His command;
to believe in the name
of His Son, Jesus Christ,
and to love one another as
He commanded us.

1 John 3:23

Scripture Cards, page 26

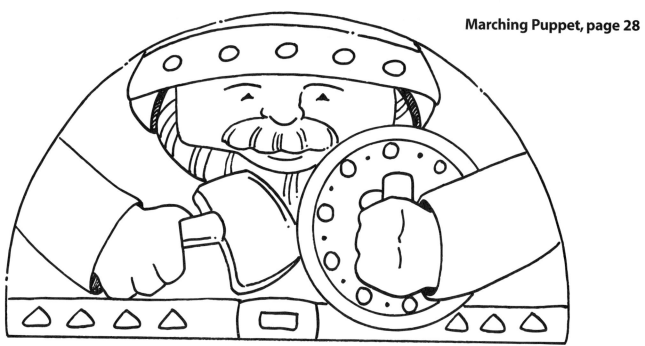

House of Obedience, page 30

As for me and my house we will serve the Lord. Joshua 24:15 (NIV)

House of Obedience, page 30

Banner of Bravery, page 32

Samuel's Bed, page 35

Nesting Dolls, page 34

When I am afraid, I will trust in you.
Psalm 56:3

cut out

Light Switch Cover, page 38

Note Holder, page 56

Naaman Puppet, page 49

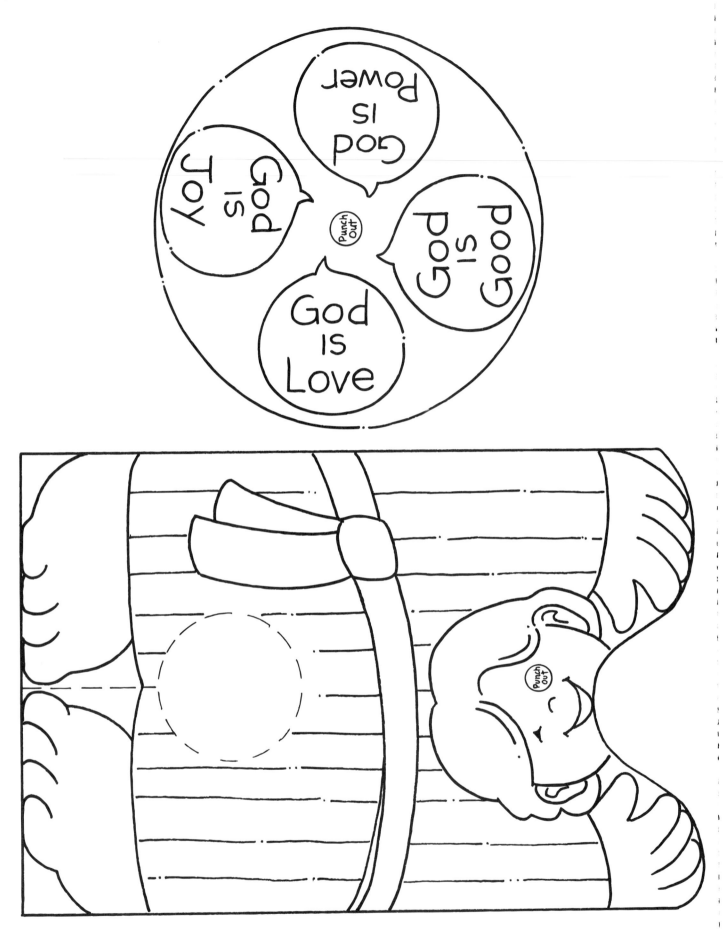

Door Hanger, page 48

Lion Puppet, page 59

Puppet Theater, page 58

1. Players sit in a circle around the spinner. Put a treat such as raisins, dry cereal, or popcorn in a bowl next to the spinner.

2. Starting with the youngest, the first player spins the spinner.

3. The first player must repeat the phrase the spinner points to and give a reason to be thankful. For instance, the first player would say, "Thank you, God, for church because I get to learn about Jesus," if the spinner was pointing to the church.

4. Each time a player tells a reason to be thankful, she gets a treat from the bowl.

5. Players take turns, going clockwise around the circle, earning treats to eat on their turns.

6. The game can be played as many times around as the players wish or until the treats are gone!

Instructions for Game of Thanks, page 67

Marionette, page 69

Doll of Myself, page 73

Offering Box, page 70

Flannel Board, page 78

Figure of Jesus for Bible, page 109

Lift-the-Flap Book, page 79

Taste and see that the Lord is good.

-Psalm 34:8

Candy Magnet, page 88

Thank
You,
Lord!

Praise Puppet, page 93

Stormy Seas, page 82

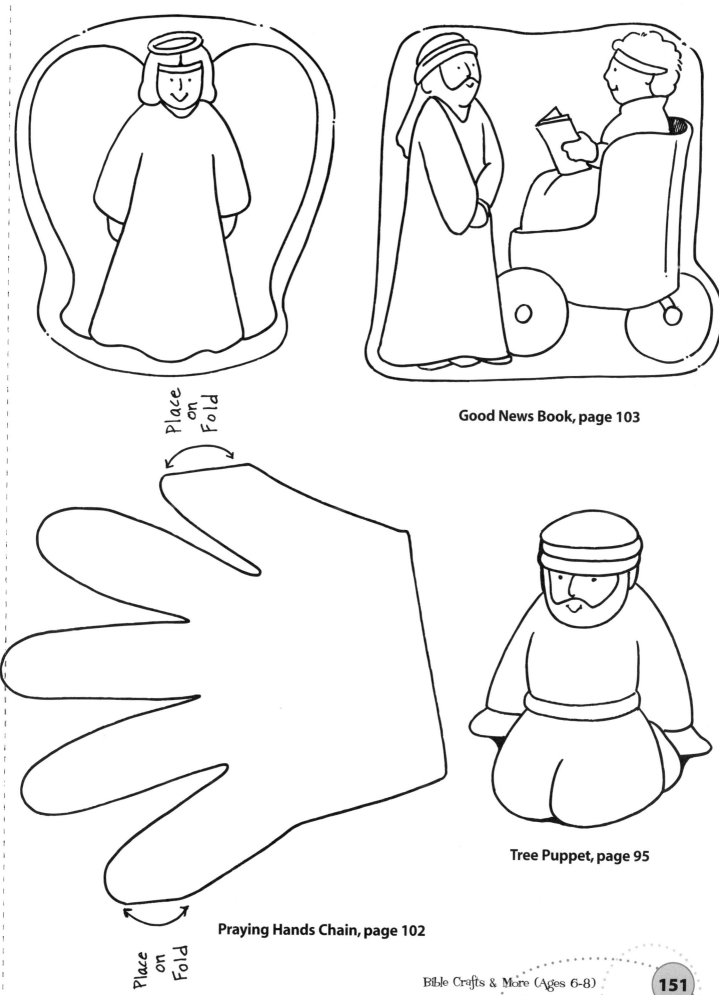

Place on Fold

Good News Book, page 103

Tree Puppet, page 95

Praying Hands Chain, page 102

Place on Fold

Leaves on a Tree, page 108

_____ (name)

I want to do good, just like Jesus.

_____ (name)

I want to love others, just like Jesus.

_____ (name)

I want to follow Jesus!

I can go to...

I can read my...

I can talk with God and...

I can listen to praise...

I can watch a Bible...

Learning Lace-up, page 105

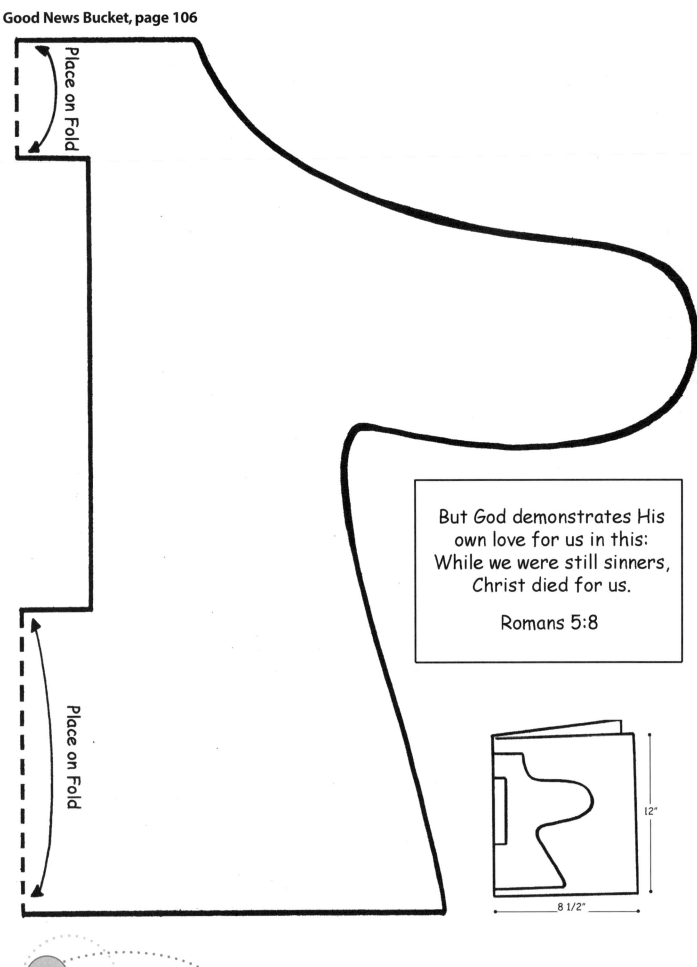

Place on Fold

Place on Fold

But God demonstrates His own love for us in this: While we were still sinners, Christ died for us.

Romans 5:8

12"

8 1/2"

Jesus is

Kind	Good	Trustworthy	Faithful	Loving	Forgiving	Our Savior	God's Son

Pull Through, page 107

Father's Day Card, page 118

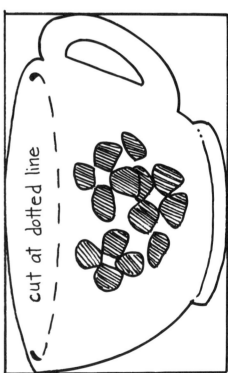

Mother's Day Card, page 116

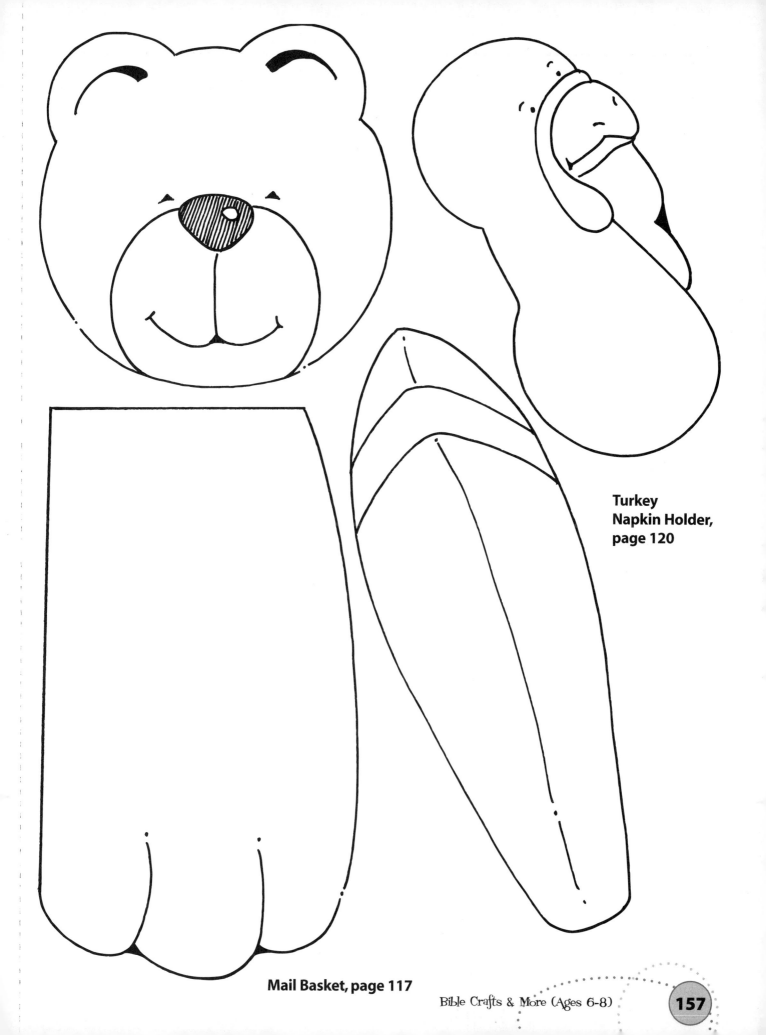

**Turkey
Napkin Holder,
page 120**

Mail Basket, page 117

Index

Index

HeartShaper™ Early Elementary Scope & Sequence

Fall Year 1
God Makes the World (p. 9)
God Makes the Animals (p. 10)
God Makes People (p. 11)
Noah Obeys God (p. 12)
God Keeps His Promise to Noah (p. 13)
Abraham's New Home (p. 14)
The Birth of Isaac (p. 16)
God Cares for Jacob (p. 19)
God Cares for Moses (p. 22)
God Cares for His People (p. 23)
God's People Cross the Red Sea (p. 24)
God Gives Food and Water (p. 25)
God Gives Ten Rules (p. 26)

Winter Year 1
An Angel Visits Mary (p. 62)
Jesus Is Born (p. 64)
Shepherds Tell Others (p. 66)
Wise Men Worship Jesus (p. 68)
Jesus Grows Up (p. 70)
Jesus Chooses Four Followers (p. 77)
Jesus and the Children (p. 94)
Jesus Brings Lazarus Back to Life (p. 92)
Jesus and the Ten Men with Leprosy (p. 93)
Jesus Is a Friend to a Woman from Samaria (p. 75)
Jesus Is a Friend to Zacchaeus (p. 95)
Jesus Is a Friend to a Woman Needing Forgiveness (p. 81)
Jesus Is a Friend to a Man Who Is Paralyzed (p. 78)

Spring Year 1
Special Unit: Jesus Is Special
The Last Supper (p. 97)
Jesus Is Alive (p. 99)
Jesus Stops a Storm (p. 82)
Jesus Heals a Man Who Can't Hear (p. 86)
Jesus Heals a Man Who Can't See (p. 88)
Paul Learns About Jesus (p. 105)
Paul and Barnabas Tell About Jesus (p. 106)
Paul and Barnabas Help People Know About Jesus (p. 107)
Lydia Follows Jesus (p. 108)
Paul and Silas Sing in Prison (p. 109)

Paul Tells a Crowd About Jesus (p. 110)
Paul Is Shipwrecked (p. 111)
Paul Tells About Jesus in Rome (p. 112)

Summer Year 1
Joshua and Caleb Believe God (p. 27)
God Is with Moses and Joshua (p. 28)
Joshua Obeys God At Jericho (p. 29)
God's People Choose to Serve Him (p. 30)
Deborah Helps Barak Obey (p. 31)
Gideon Is Brave (p. 32)
Ruth Works Hard (p. 33)
Jonah Changes His Mind (p. 60)
Hannah Keeps a Promise (p. 34)
Samuel Listens and Obeys (p. 35)
Samuel Obeys God (p. 36)
Saul Disobeys God (p. 37)
Samuel Anoints David as King (p. 38)

Fall Year 2
David Does His Job (p. 39)
David Is Brave (p. 40)
David and Jonathan are Friends (p. 41)
David Does the Right Thing (p. 42)
God Cares for Elijah (p. 44)
God Gives Elijah Food (p. 45)
God Shows His Power Through Elijah (p. 46)
God Brings a Boy Back to Life (p. 48)
God Heals an Obedient Naaman (p. 49)
Solomon Prays for Wisdom (p. 43)
Hezekiah Prays for Healing (p. 50)
Jehoshaphat Prays for Help (p. 52)
Manasseh Prays for Forgiveness (p. 53)

Winter Year 2
Zechariah Praises God (p. 61)
Mary Sings to God (p. 63)
Shepherds Tell About Jesus' Birth (p. 65)
Simeon and Anna Thank God (p. 67)
Wise Men Worship Jesus (p. 69)
John Baptizes Jesus (p. 71)
Satan Tempts Jesus (p. 72)
Jesus' First Followers (p. 73)
Jesus with Moses and Elijah (p. 87)
Jesus Teaches About Prayer (p. 90)
Jesus Teaches About Sharing (p. 91)

Jesus Teaches About Helping (p. 89)
Jesus Teaches About God (p. 74)

Spring Year 2
Special Unit: Jesus Is Special
People Praise Jesus (p. 96)
Jesus Dies and Lives Again (p. 98)
Jesus Heals an Official's Son (p. 76)
Jesus Heals a Man at a Pool (p. 79)
Jesus Feeds 5,000 (p. 84)
Jesus Walks on Water (p. 85)
Jesus Brings a Young Man Back to Life (p. 80)
Jesus Heals Jairus's Daughter (p. 83)
The Church Begins (p. 100)
Peter and John at the Temple (p. 101)
Peter and John Speak Boldly (p. 102)
Philip Teaches a Man from Ethiopia (p. 103)
Peter and Tabitha (p. 104)

Summer Year 2
Abraham Lets Lot Choose First (p. 15)
Rebekah Is Kind (p. 17)
Isaac Is a Peacemaker (p. 18)
Joseph Does His Best (p. 20)
Joseph Forgives His Brothers (p. 21)
Micaiah Tells the Truth (p. 47)
King Josiah Obeys the Law (p. 51)
Queen Esther Helps Others (p. 55)
Ezra and Nehemiah Help the People Do Right (p. 54)
Job Does What Is Right (p. 56)
Daniel and His Friends Eat Good Food (p. 57)
Daniel's Friends Face a Fiery Furnace (p. 58)
Daniel and the Lions' Den (p. 59)